W9-API-680

Dear Valued Customer,

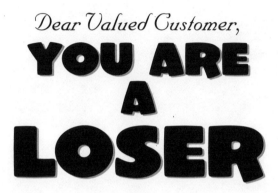

Dear Valued Customer,

YOU ARE A LOSER

And Over 100 Other Embarrassing and Funny Stories of Technology Gone Mad

RICK BROADHEAD

Andrews McMeel
Publishing

Kansas City

CONTENTS

Acknowledgments . . . ix

Introduction . . . xi

PART 1

E-MAIL GAGS AND GAFFES . . . 1

PART 2

BANKING BLUNDERS AND FINANCIAL FLUBS . . . 45

PART 3

BUSINESS BLOOPERS, HIGH·TECH HOAXES, AND MEDICAL MIRACLES . . . 83

PART 4

TELECOM SNAFUS . . . 149

PART 5

MEDIA MISTAKES AND MISHAPS . . . 179

PART 6

GOVERNMENT GLITCHES, GOOFS, AND GAGS . . . 239

PART 7

MISCELLANEOUS MARVELS, FANTASTIC FEATS, AND OTHER ODDITIES . . . 285

ACKNOWLEDGMENTS

A warm thank-you to Patty Rice at Andrews McMeel for believing in this book and for her invaluable suggestions; to my agents, Kim Witherspoon and Alexis Hurley, for sharing their professional advice and acting as my sounding board; to Jim Carroll for giving me my start in publishing; and to Mom, Dad, Lionel, and Kristin for their unwavering love and support.

INTRODUCTION

Welcome to the inaugural edition of *Dear Valued Customer, You Are a Loser,* a humorous celebration of the unintended consequences of modern, everyday technology.

I've long been a fan of books like *Ripley's Believe It or Not* and the *Guinness Book of World Records,* and this book was born out of my attempts to document and catalog some of the strangest and most memorable technological oddities of all time.

Most of the stories presented here describe humorous, bizarre, or unfortunate incidents that were to some degree caused or facilitated by technology. For good measure, I've also included some classic hoaxes and other offbeat stories that have earned their own unique place in history. Incredible as they may seem, all of the stories are true unless otherwise indicated.

I've decided to open the book with the story of two Seattle businessmen, Shane Atchison and Tom Farmer (www.zaaz.com), who rocked the business world with their widely circulated PowerPoint presentation called "Yours Is a Very Bad Hotel." After receiving a rude reception at an upscale hotel in Houston, Shane and Tom created the presentation as a creative way to vent their frustration and express their anger at the way they were treated. The graphic complaint was forwarded to the hotel's manager and a few of Shane's and Tom's close friends, but it unexpectedly got passed around by e-mail and quickly found a worldwide audience on the Internet, much to the dismay of the hotel's management. Shane and Tom have kindly given their permission for several of their infamous slides to be reproduced in this book. I hope you laugh as hard as I did when I first came across their incredible story.

PART 1

E·MAIL GAGS
AND GAFFES

Shane Atchison and Tom Farmer of Seattle, Washington, are heroes to customer service advocates everywhere. After receiving shabby service at a major hotel, the two business executives fought back and won, proving that customers everywhere have more power than they realize. All it takes is a bit of creativity.

HEARTBREAK HOTEL

Shane Atchison and Tom Farmer, November 2001

In November 2001, Atchison and Farmer flew from Seattle to Texas for a business trip. They had a guaranteed reservation at an upscale hotel in Houston, but when they showed up at the front desk at 2 A.M., weary after a long plane ride, they discovered their room had been given away earlier in the evening.

To make matters worse, they were greeted by an unsympathetic and unapologetic desk clerk named Mike.

Fuming with anger, Shane and Tom vented their frustration in a rather unconventional way—they created a seventeen-slide PowerPoint

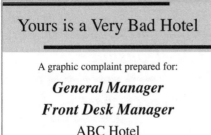

Yours is a Very Bad Hotel

A graphic complaint prepared for:

General Manager
Front Desk Manager
ABC Hotel
Houston, Texas

presentation about the manner in which they were treated and promptly e-mailed it to the hotel and several of their friends. The presentation was humorously titled "Yours Is a Very Bad Hotel."

The original slides contained the actual name of the establishment, but it was later removed and replaced with "ABC Hotel" to give the hotel some much-needed anonymity.

The PowerPoint presentation contained a variety of witty slides, including one depicting the career path of the unhelpful desk clerk who

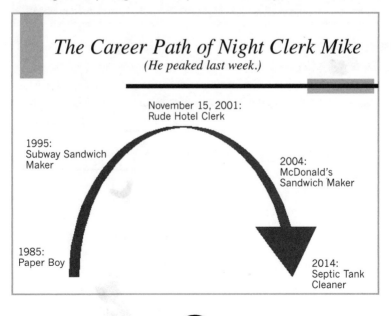

The Career Path of Night Clerk Mike
(He peaked last week.)

November 15, 2001:
Rude Hotel Clerk

1995:
Subway Sandwich Maker

2004:
McDonald's
Sandwich Maker

1985:
Paper Boy

2014:
Septic Tank
Cleaner

We Are Very Unlikely to Return to the ABC Hotel Houston.

Lifetime chances of dying in a bathtub: **1 in 10,455**

(National Safety Council)

Chance of Earth being ejected from the solar system by the gravitational pull of a passing star: **1 in 2,200,000**

(University of Michigan)

Chance of winning the UK Lottery: **1 in 13,983,816**

(UK Lottery)

Chance of us returning to the ABC Hotel Houston: **worse than any of those**

(And what are the chances you'd save rooms for us anyway?)

greeted them at the hotel in the wee hours of that November morning. There was also a dictionary definition of the word "guarantee," quotes from the unapologetic desk clerk, an entertaining display of probability statistics, and a bar graph illustrating the amount of money that Shane and Tom's firm shelled out annually for hotel accommodations in the Houston area.

Shane's and Tom's friends were so impressed with the PowerPoint slides that they couldn't resist e-mailing them to *their* friends. In turn, those

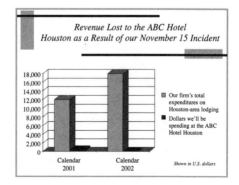

Revenue Lost to the ABC Hotel Houston as a Result of our November 15 Incident

- Our firm's total expenditures on Houston-area lodging
- Dollars we'll be spending at the ABC Hotel Houston

Calendar 2001   Calendar 2002

Shown in U.S. dollars

> **In the Early Morning Hours of**
> **November 15, 2001, at the ABC Hotel Houston,**
> **We Were Treated Very Badly Indeed.**
>
> - We are Tom Farmer and Shane Atchison of Seattle, Washington.
> - We held guaranteed, confirmed reservations at the ABC Hotel for the night of November 14-15.
> - These rooms were held for late arrival with a major credit card.
> - Tom is a card-carrying Frequent Guest at ABC Hotel . . .
> - Yet when we arrived at 2:00am. . . *we were refused rooms!*

friends e-mailed the presentation to *their* friends, and so on. You can guess what happened next.

Within hours, Shane and Tom's PowerPoint slides had circulated around the globe and were eliciting howls of laughter from readers. As the presentation traveled from one inbox to the next, Tom began receiving hundreds of e-mail messages from admirers and supporters all over the world. At one point, Tom had 1,000 e-mail messages in his inbox from people on five continents. They included business travelers who sympathized with the pair's plight, business professors who wanted to use the slides in their lectures as an example of how *not* to treat customers, and average people who simply wanted to cheer Shane and Tom on in their battle against an unrepentant hotel chain.

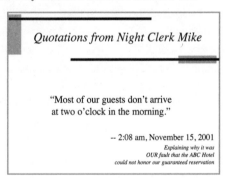

> *Quotations from Night Clerk Mike*
>
> "Most of our guests don't arrive at two o'clock in the morning."
>
> -- 2:08 am, November 15, 2001
> *Explaining why it was*
> *OUR fault that the ABC Hotel*
> *could not honor our guaranteed reservation*

Included in the e-mail "blizzard" were several heartwarming messages. One woman, who had been trapped in the World Trade Center during the horrific events of September 11, e-mailed Tom to say the PowerPoint slides made her laugh for the first time in three months.

"Everyone but the penguins had checked in," explained Tom in a telephone interview where he described the incredible turn of events.

The Experience Mike Provided Deviated from Usual Treatment of a Frequent Guest Member.

Expected Frequent Guest Member Benefits	Actual Benefits Provided by ABC Hotel 11/15
Confirmed reservation	Ignored reservation
Upgraded room when available	No room available
Free continental breakfast	Free confusing directions to shabby alternate hotel
Frequent Guest Member benefits	Insolence *plus* insults

He even received e-mail messages from women asking if he was single.

Ironically, the hotel in Houston hadn't been able to open the PowerPoint presentation, so they were oblivious to the worldwide frenzy their customer service gaffe had created.

However, it didn't take long for the hotel to learn of the presentation's existence. Many of the people who had received the PowerPoint presentation reportedly picked up the phone and personally called the hotel to express their disgust over the way Shane and Tom had been treated.

Copies of the presentation eventually found their way into the hands of the media, and several papers—including the prestigious *Wall Street Journal*—wrote about the incident. Not surprisingly, several competing hotel chains also took advantage of the story and offered gift certificates to both Shane and Tom.

As for the hotel in Houston that had sparked this unique form of customer protest, they were extremely remorseful once they learned what had happened. Recognizing that they were now under an unwanted national spotlight, both the hotel's general manager and a brand manager from the chain personally called Shane and Tom to apologize. By this time, the hotel was being inundated with calls, so they were ready to do just about anything to get Shane and Tom to call off their troops.

To demonstrate they were taking the complaints seriously, the chain sent Shane and Tom a list of actions taken at both the corporate and hotel levels to prevent a similar situation from arising in the future. In

We Discussed With Mike the Meaning of the Term "Guarantee."

guar·an·tee (gar-ən-tē), *n.*

- Something that assures a particular outcome or condition: *Lack of interest is a guarantee of failure.*
    - A promise or an assurance, especially one given in writing, that attests to the quality or durability of a product or service.
    - A pledge that something will be performed in a specified manner.

(Save this for your future reference.)

addition, both the hotel and its corporate headquarters agreed to make sizable contributions to a local Houston charity—the Houston Toys for Tots campaign—at Shane and Tom's request.

"We've made our point beyond our wildest dreams," said Tom. "We never dreamed the presentation would get passed around like this. Every crisis is a brand-building opportunity and this whole incident is a testament to the viral power of e-mail."

Sources: Tom Farmer, *National Post, USA Today, Wall Street Journal,* ZAAZ Inc.

> Imagine learning that someone had secretly been intercepting your e-mail messages for months, quietly removing certain words and putting synonyms in their place. Imagine if hundreds of thousands of Internet users were victims of the same mischievous practice.

NOT YOUR AVERAGE COFFEE FILTER

Yahoo!, July 2002

Incredible as it sounds, it's true. It came to light in 2002 that Yahoo!, one of the largest providers of Web-based e-mail services in the world, had secretly been exchanging certain words in the e-mail messages sent by their customers.

Yahoo!'s bizarre actions might have escaped detection had the company not targeted a few common words that frequently appeared in people's e-mail correspondence. For example, in a move that no doubt offended coffee drinkers everywhere, Yahoo! began zapping the word "mocha" from e-mail messages and silently replacing it with the word "espresso."

Even word fragments couldn't escape Yahoo!'s wrath. For example, whenever Yahoo! encountered the letter combination "eval" in an e-mail message, it would automatically be changed to "review." So the word "evaluation" would be changed to "reviewuation" and "medieval" would appear as "medireview."

With hundreds of thousands of people using Yahoo!'s e-mail services, the impact of this kind of word-tinkering was widespread. Nonsensical words began to pop up in academic papers, newspaper articles, and business documents. Indeed, anything that passed through Yahoo!'s e-mail filter before being posted on the Web was at the mercy of Yahoo!'s automated censors.

You can see Yahoo!'s handiwork for yourself on the Google search engine. For example, a search for the nonexistent word "reviewuation" yields hundreds of matches. And because the word "prevalent" (containing the taboo word fragment "eval") would be automatically changed by Yahoo! to "prreviewent," the Internet is full of incomprehensible sentences like "The despair you're feeling is so prreviewent."

What did Yahoo! have to say for themselves? They explained that the word modification was necessary to prevent hackers from using a computer language called Web scripting to steal passwords and commit other types of cyber crimes. While some of the commands in Web scripting are obscure computer-specific words, others are common everyday words like "mocha" and "expression." Yahoo! was worried that a hacker could slip the dangerous computer commands into an e-mail message and use them to launch an attack on someone, so they created a blacklist of words that posed a potential security risk. Yahoo! began zapping the subversive words from e-mail messages passing through their system and replacing them with less-threatening words—thus, "mocha" became "espresso," and the word "expression" was replaced with "statement."

Despite Yahoo!'s seemingly honorable intentions, many people were furious that the company had for months been modifying the content of their e-mail messages without telling them. But for those with a sense of humor, there are some hilariously funny examples of the havoc Yahoo!'s filter caused.

One user complained that Yahoo!'s unconventional practices had caused her extreme embarrassment. "As the director of a political group, it is extremely frustrating to use 'freedom of expression' and have it come up 'freedom of statement!'" the exasperated woman wrote in a message posted on the Internet. "I sent e-mail out to an entire e-mail list and sounded like an idiot!"

Sources: *National Post,* News.com, *New York Times,* Reuters

isdirected e-mail can have amusing or dire consequences. This is the story of one of the biggest e-mail screwups I've ever come across.

CLICK HERE TO GO TO JAIL

IDEXX Laboratories, January 1998

In January 1998, a woman named Caryn was unhappily working as a chemist at IDEXX Laboratories in Maine, a leading supplier of diagnostic products and services for the veterinary industry. One day while scouring employment opportunities on the Internet, she came across a competing company called Wyoming DNAVaccine.

Caryn became interested in possibly working for Wyoming, so she e-mailed her résumé to the company. Wyoming's chief scientific officer, whom we'll call Stephen, responded positively to Caryn's inquiry, and the two started corresponding by e-mail.

Initially, the pair exchanged a lot of information about their personal lives, but eventually Stephen began to ask Caryn for confidential information pertaining to IDEXX's business. Although Caryn was initially reluctant to supply proprietary information to a competitor, she eventually began e-mailing Stephen all kinds of sensitive material, including customer lists, manufacturing documents, and laboratory files. She also tipped Stephen off about a possible acquisition that was in the works.

Stephen was allegedly planning to use the information to compete against IDEXX. In exchange for Caryn's espionage work, he apparently promised her a position in the new company, even hinting that she could be the CEO one day. Caryn seemed to enjoy her new pastime, even remarking to Stephen at one point, "Aren't I awful? I'm liking this spy business way too much."

On July 24, as Caryn prepared to go to California and meet Stephen for the first time, she mailed him two boxes full of top-secret data, including operating manuals and research and development information. That night, Caryn wrote Stephen an e-mail describing the seven binders' worth of stolen material that was coming his way. "There's some really cool stuff coming through," she wrote. "You'll feel like a kid on Christmas day!"

In her excitement, however, Caryn made a horrible mistake. When she went into her computer's address book to send the message to Stephen, she mistakenly selected the address for John Lawrence, IDEXX's global marketing director, and the incriminating message went to Lawrence instead.

Caryn immediately realized the enormity of her mistake. She wrote a second e-mail to Stephen and told him what had just happened. "I just screwed up," she said. "I think the biggest screwup of my life. And I can't stop shaking, I'm so scared."

We can only imagine the look on John Lawrence's face when he opened his e-mail and saw Caryn bragging about her espionage work. Lawrence quickly notified the authorities, and Caryn was summarily fired from her job at IDEXX. After agreeing to testify against Stephen, she was sentenced to three years' probation.

As for Stephen, he served a year in prison after becoming only the second person in U.S. history brought to trial under the U.S. Economic Espionage Act of 1996. He is now spending his time working on a cure for cancer. Stephen is also taking advantage of his unique experience and warning businesses about the pitfalls of corresponding on-line. To that end, he has released a list of tips to help people steer clear of trouble when using electronic mail. It is aptly titled "How to E-Mail Yourself to Hell and/or Federal Prison with Only the Click of a Mouse."

Sources: Associated Press, *San Francisco Chronicle*,
U.S. Department of Justice Web site (usdoj.gov)

There are lots of stories about private e-mail accidentally getting into the wrong hands and becoming fodder for tabloids and major newspapers alike. The following true story, which originated in New York City, is about as embarrassing as it gets.

SEX IN THE CITY

New York City, September 2002

This tale begins in late August 2002, when "Tripp," an investment banker in New York, met "Mary," an employee at PricewaterhouseCoopers, a consulting firm. The week after their initial encounter, Tripp sent Mary a friendly e-mail, in an apparent attempt to strike up some conversation. This is what he wrote:

So are you off to the Bon Jovi show tonight in Times Square? Sounds like it is going to some turnout. What division of audit are you in for PWC? Are you heading out tonight? A friend of mine is leaving for MBA School in France so, he is throwing himself a going away party at Park, ever been? What are the

plans for this weekend, recovery from the long weekend or adding just a little more hurt to the situation?

Upon receiving the e-mail, Mary decided to forward the message to a friend, along with some intimate details about her personal life. She disclosed how another acquaintance of hers had fallen asleep during sex the night before, and how Tripp would probably do anything to get her into bed. Here is what Mary wrote:

"Ok first-here is the e-mail I received from Tripp, the new guy I met last week. If you want to go out, perhaps we can get him to pay for drinks at Park. Since we have not slept together, he will of course be trying to impress me and will, therefore, do anything I ask. Unlike John, who fell asleep during sex last night. I went over to his place last night around 11:30. We started having sex. When I noticed his eyes were closed for a little too long, I said 'John wake up.' At which, point he shot up saying 'what'd I miss.' Yes, I think that is a new low."

Little did Mary know that she was about to hit yet another new low. Instead of clicking on "Forward" to send the message to her friend, she had clicked on "Reply" and accidentally sent the message to Tripp.

Tripp got the message and no doubt was amused by its contents. Without skipping a beat, he forwarded the misdirected e-mail to some of his friends with the message, "You will love this."

You can imagine what happened next. Some of Tripp's friends forwarded the message to their friends, who in turn forwarded it to their friends, and so on. Mary's e-mail traveled the world faster than a speeding bullet and became a hot topic of conversation around water coolers across the nation. As the correspondence was zapped from one inbox to the next, people added messages like, "Read this. You will love it," and "Drop what you are doing and read this. The following is an exchange between a friend of a guy that sits on our desk and a girl he took out on a date. Read from the bottom up. Oh my lord."

Many people realized how Mary's misfortune could have easily happened to them. "I laughed when I first read it," said one executive interviewed by the *National Post*. "You could totally see how someone could have made that mistake. I have a personal contact list of 700 people. It took me about two seconds to forward it to 30 people."

As the e-mail made its way around the world, Mary became a poster child for New York women. "I forwarded the e-mail to friends too, to show them that that stuff happens," said another recipient of the errant e-mail interviewed by the *National Post*. "I lived and worked in New York and none of my friends would believe it when I would tell them nutty stories about New York women like that. This shows it happens."

Mary never commented publicly about her ordeal, and given the embarrassing nature of the incident, PricewaterhouseCoopers said they weren't going to discipline Mary in any way. Indeed, the humiliation she had suffered was punishment enough.

Sources: *Daily Mirror* (United Kingdom),
e-mail correspondence, *National Post*

When Washington, D.C., radio station Z104 teamed up with Starbucks to promote the coffee chain's new Frappuccino beverage, they had no idea their regional promotion would quickly turn into a national news story.

FRAPPUCCINO FRENZY

Starbucks Coffee Company, July 2002

The marketing blitz began in July 2002 when Z104 mailed out free Frappuccino coupons to 5,000 of the station's listeners. All was going well until one mischievous listener received the mouthwatering offer in the mail and decided to have a bit of fun at Starbucks' expense. The prankster scanned the coupon into his computer, electronically altered it, and started forwarding it to people by e-mail. Of course, once the coupon was tossed into cyberspace, it spread faster than a prairie brushfire.

Not realizing the coupon was a fake, hundreds of Frappuccino addicts and coffee lovers printed the coupon and rushed to their nearest Starbucks location in anticipation of their complimentary coffees.

Compounding matters further, many people forwarded the coupon to their friends, who in turn forwarded it to their friends, and so on, creating what one newspaper called "the Frappuccino effect."

Many Starbucks locations, unaware that the offer was phony, redeemed the coupon and granted the free drink to throngs of delighted customers. In some stores, Starbucks employees faced a stampede of coupon holders. "We went through hell [Tuesday] for four hours," said an employee interviewed by the *New York Post*. "There were people coming ten at a time."

In one location, the horde of coupon-wielding customers sucked the store dry of its entire supply of Vanilla Creme Frappuccinos. "We gave away lots and lots of them [Tuesday] because we didn't know," said a Starbucks server interviewed by the *Washington Post*. "It's hard to believe this is real. We've run out of the Vanilla Creme Frappuccinos. It's all gone."

When Starbucks' head office finally got wind of the cyber scheme, they alerted store managers and warned them not to accept any more of the bogus coupons. While many customers took the prank in stride, some die-hard coffee drinkers got really stirred up by the bad news. "I can't tell you how many times I've been cussed out today," complained a flustered Starbucks employee to the *Washington Post*. "Some people are getting really mad even when I explain it to them."

While Starbucks won't reveal how much money they lost as a result of the scam, there's no doubt that the counterfeit coupons and the subsequent media attention had the effect of increasing demand for Starbucks Frappuccinos across the country. As the saying goes, you can't buy publicity like that!

Sources: *New York Post, San Francisco Chronicle,* Starbucks, *Toronto Star, Washington Post*

> How many lawyers does it take to foul up a confidential e-mail? Just one, apparently, if the law firm is New York's Weil, Gotshal & Manges.

SO MUCH FOR LAWYER·CLIENT PRIVILEGE

Weil, Gotshal & Manges, March 2002

On March 28, 2002, a lawyer at the firm, one of the world's largest, was preparing an e-mail to a list of more than fifty companies that had confidentially expressed interest in purchasing the assets of bankrupt telecommunications firm Global Crossing. Weil, Gotshal & Manges was sending out the e-mail because it had been retained by Global Crossing to assist the company with its bankruptcy proceedings.

The lawyer composing the e-mail, however, apparently wasn't paying close enough attention to what he or she was doing. Rather than use the "blind carbon copy" feature that is common to most e-mail programs, the lawyer put the e-mail addresses of all the confidential bidders in the "To:" line of the e-mail message, where they could be seen by all the recipients.

The e-mail message, with all the confidential names listed in it, was subsequently obtained by the *New York Times,* which then recounted the lawyer's goof in a news story. On their Web site, the *New York Times* went even further and actually published the entire contents of the e-mail message along with the e-mail addresses of all the potential bidders.

The e-mail, besides being a major embarrassment for Weil, Gotshal & Manges, became the subject of much gossip on Wall Street, since it revealed the secret identities of companies who might be interested in buying Global Crossing's assets. The list of recipients included telecommunications giants such as Verizon, the BT Group, Deutsche Telekom, Telefónica of Spain, and Teléfonos de Mexico (Telmex), as well as financial powerhouses like Credit Suisse First Boston, Bank One, and the Canadian Imperial Bank of Commerce.

Having apparently just botched one of the biggest bankruptcies in U.S. history, Weil, Gotshal & Manges was asked what they had to say for themselves. Their response? "No comment."

Source: *New York Times*

> f you're going to throw a temper tantrum, it's wise
> to do it when you're away from your computer.

TEMPER TANTRUM

Cerner Corporation, March 2001

case in point is the amusing story of Neal Patterson, the founder and longtime CEO of Cerner Corporation, one of the world's leading health-care-technology firms. Patterson's mince-no-words management style got him into trouble in 2001 when he distributed a biting e-mail to his staff without thinking about the consequences. Patterson's e-mail and the corporate chaos that followed quickly became a classic textbook case of the perils of business e-mail.

On March 13, 2001, when this story begins, Cerner Corporation was enjoying a run as one of the best-performing stocks on the NASDAQ. The company had also made *Fortune Magazine*'s 2000 list of the 100 best companies to work for in America. Moreover, that particular day in

March, Cerner was basking in the glow of a full-page advertisement they had taken out in the *Wall Street Journal* to raise their profile on Wall Street. It seemed that things could only get better for the company.

But when Neal Patterson arrived for work early that morning, everything was about to take a turn for the worse.

Cerner had 3,100 employees worldwide, with about 2,000 working in Kansas City. On this particular Tuesday morning, Patterson decided that his troops weren't working hard enough, so the fifty-one-year-old CEO went into his office and sent an angry e-mail to approximately 400 company managers, blaming them for the company's poor work ethic and threatening to fire them if the situation didn't improve quickly.

In his scathing memo, Patterson blasted his managers for allowing employees to think they had to work only forty hours a week. "We are getting less than 40 hours of work from a large number of our K.C.-based EMPLOYEES," the memo read. "The parking lot is sparsely used at 8 A.M.; likewise at 5 P.M. As managers—you either do not know what your EMPLOYEES are doing; or you do not CARE. You have created expectations on the work effort which allowed this to happen inside Cerner, creating a very unhealthy environment. In either case, you have a problem and you will fix it or I will replace you."

Patterson also threatened to implement a wide variety of disciplinary measures, including installing time clocks, discontinuing an employee stock discount program, and cutting staff by 5 percent, if employees didn't start working harder immediately. "Hell will freeze over before this CEO implements ANOTHER EMPLOYEE benefit in this Culture," Patterson wrote. "I think this parental type action SUCKS. However, what you are doing, as managers, with this company makes me SICK."

The memo ended with Patterson giving his managers an ultimatum: "I am giving you two weeks to fix this. My measurement will be the parking lot: it should be substantially full at 7:30 AM and 6:30 P.M. The pizza man should show up at 7:30 P.M. to feed the starving teams working late. The lot should be half full on Saturday mornings. We have a lot of work to do. If you do not have enough to keep your teams busy, let me know immediately…You have two weeks. Tick, tock."

What happened next is unprecedented in the history of business. On March 21, eight days after Patterson circulated the memo, an anonymous person took the memo and posted it on an on-line message board on Yahoo!, one of the most popular Web sites in the world.

Patterson's once-private e-mail was now public, and the harsh tone of the memo stunned financial analysts, investors, and the entire business community.

Rumors began to circulate that the company was in deep trouble. Some people surmised that Patterson was panicking because the company was in danger of missing their target for first-quarter earnings.

Analysts, who began receiving calls from worried investors, began calling Cerner, seeking confirmation that the e-mail was authentic.

Many people naturally assumed the whole incident was a hoax. After all, no CEO in their right mind would have sent out an inflammatory e-mail like this, would they? But the memo wasn't a hoax and the real fallout hadn't even begun.

The very next day, investors began to hammer Cerner's stock. Cerner's trading volume, which typically averaged about 650,000 shares a day, reached 1.2 million shares.

On Friday, March 23, 4 million shares in Cerner exchanged hands— almost *four times* the normal trading volume for a Friday. In just a few days, the company's stock price had plummeted by $10 and $270 million had been wiped off Cerner's market capitalization.

Patterson's personal wealth was hit equally hard. As Cerner's stock took a nosedive, the CEO personally lost about $28 million.

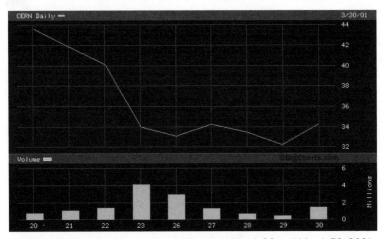

Cerner's stock price and trading volume between March 20 and March 30, 2001. The stock plummeted after a harsh letter from CEO Neal Patterson became public.

The company immediately moved into damage control, issuing a press release in an attempt to defuse the situation and assure investors that the company was on track with their expected first-quarter earnings.

Patterson, meanwhile, sent a memo to employees apologizing for his e-mail rant that had offended some employees but also reiterating his belief that there was a productivity problem within the company.

In an interview with the *New York Times,* Patterson said his direct management style stemmed from his upbringing on a farm in Oklahoma. "You can take the boy off the farm, but you can't take the farm out of the boy," he said. Patterson also stated that he deliberately exaggerated in the controversial memo in order to make a point and encourage discussion. He said he had no plans to carry out any of the threats listed in the message.

Reflecting on his actions, Patterson seemed to express some regret that he had ever sent the e-mail in the first place—an error in judgment that was compounded by the global nature of e-mail. "I was trying to start a fire," he said to the *New York Times*. "I lit a match, and I started a firestorm."

Fortunately for Patterson, the firestorm eventually blew over, Cerner's stock gradually recovered, and Patterson was able to remain at the helm of the company he had founded. "Everyone has sent an e-mail that they regret, but as far as I know, no one has had one circulated around the world in this way," said a Cerner spokesperson quoted in *The Times* (London). "Neal has said he will think twice in the future before hitting the send button."

Sources: *Fortune* magazine, *Globe and Mail, Kansas City Star, New York Times, Times* (London)

> any people have made the mistake of sending an e-mail message they later regretted. But few such incidents can top what happened to a twenty-four-year-old Princeton graduate we'll call Peter.

WHAT GOES AROUND COMES AROUND

The Carlyle Group, Seoul, South Korea, May 2001

n 2001, Peter was on top of the world, having just moved to Seoul, South Korea, where he had accepted a job as an associate with the Carlyle Group, a private equity firm. But on May 15, 2001, he made an error in judgment that he will no doubt remember for the rest of his life.

On that day, Peter sent out a brash e-mail to several of his friends and former colleagues, bragging about his new job and the incredible perks that came with it. In the e-mail, Peter boasted about his sexual escapades and asked his friends to send him boxes of condoms to replenish his low supply. "I brought out about 40," he wrote, "but I think I'll run out of them by Saturday."

"I know I was a stud in NYC but I pretty much get about, on average, 5-8 phone numbers a night and at least 3 hot chicks that say that they want to go home with me every night I go out," the e-mail read.

Peter also boasted about his vast living quarters. "I've got a spanking brand new 2000 sq. foot 3 bedroom apt. with a 200 sq. foot terrace running the entire length of my apartment with a view overlooking Korea's main river and nightline," he wrote. He explained that one of the three bedrooms was reserved for his sexual encounters with women, while another was for his "harem of chickies."

"I have bankers calling me everyday with opportunities and they pretty much cater to my every whim - you know (golfing events, lavish dinners, a night out clubbing)," he crowed.

It doesn't take much imagination to figure out what happened next. Some of Peter's colleagues who received the e-mail forwarded the e-mail to their friends, who in turn passed it on to their friends, and so on. Before long, Peter's message was being read by thousands of people on Wall Street and his once-promising career began to unravel.

As might be expected, Peter's e-mail eventually appeared on the desks of his bosses at the Carlyle Group, who confronted the hapless stud and gave him the choice of resigning or being fired.

By that time, the e-mail message had been read by so many people on Wall Street that the *New York Times* wrote a story about it, giving Peter even more unwanted publicity.

The e-mail message, along with the trail of comments from everyone whose computer it passed through, made for hilarious reading, but for Peter, it was a major embarrassment. When reached in Seoul by the *New York Times,* he described the ordeal as "devastating."

One financial executive who fowarded Peter's e-mail to his colleagues—prior to the *New York Times* story—added the following warning: "Rule No. 1 we learned in IB training: If you don't want it published in the NYT, don't write it."

Sources: *New York Post, New York Times*

When AT&T implemented a new junk e-mail filter for their Internet subscribers, customers rejoiced. They hoped the new software would put an end to the never-ending streams of junk mail, or spam, they were receiving. But the software ended up being a double-edged sword for AT&T. In May 2002, the company discovered that the software was blocking their own e-mail messages to customers.

TOO SMART FOR ITS OWN GOOD

AT&T Corporation, May 2002

The company became aware of the problem after they e-mailed a rate increase to subscribers and then heard from several customers who claimed they had never received the notice. AT&T promptly did a test of the e-mail filter and found the source of the problem was their own software.

A spokesperson for AT&T tried to put a humorous spin on the glitch. "If there is a silver lining, it appears our spam-filtering system works so well that it even deletes mass e-mails from our own company," he said.

Sources: Associated Press, Silicon.com

Kevin Hendershot of Toronto, Canada, was planning a dream vacation with his wife to the exotic South Pacific island of Palau, a world-renowned diving destination near the Philippines. Although Palau was his destination of choice, he was concerned about the weather. Kevin had little flexibility in departure dates because of his wife's work schedule, and the only time the couple could go was in late July/early August 2002, right in the middle of Palau's wet season. Although Kevin had been assured by tourism officials on the island that the weather would be fine, there was still a slight risk of a typhoon hitting the island during their stay.

THE ELDERS ARE GETTING RESTLESS

Toronto, Ontario, Canada, July 2002

As the couple's vacation drew closer, Kevin's nerves were increasingly frayed as he debated whether the trip to Palau was worth taking. With visions of hurricane-force winds dancing in his head, he began considering alternate destinations where the weather wouldn't be an issue. It was during this tense period leading up to the couple's departure that a close friend of Kevin's decided to play a practical joke on them. The friend knew Kevin was planning to stay at a bed-and-breakfast resort on Palau called Carolines, so he forged an e-mail message to make it look like it had come from resort, and made a plea on behalf of the governor of Palau. Here is what the message said:

To: Kevin Hendershot
From: Carolines
Subject: Request from Carolines

Kevin:

We are looking forward to seeing you in a few weeks. I feel uncomfortable asking you this, but you were asking about typhoons and we recently had an appeal from the Governor of Palau. Many of the residents go to the outer islands during June and July to avoid the storms on the main island. We are short a couple of volunteers for early August who can be on call to help some of the elder island residents should a major typhoon come to the island. We can make due without the help of tourists, but it always helps to have a few extra hands if we need them. All that is required is that you be willing to help if we need you. We would give you a pager and two-way radio. We would probably only need you for one of the two weeks you will be staying with us. The Governor would be grateful for your help.

Zenie

When Kevin received the request, he was exasperated. This was not what he had signed up for. The last thing he wanted to do on his vacation was to wear a pager and be on call throughout the night to rescue elderly island residents in distress. Then again, how do you say no to the governor? Kevin immediately forwarded the message to his better half and replied back to Carolines saying he would need to discuss the matter with his wife.

Meanwhile, Kevin's friend was on pins and needles waiting for Kevin to call and tell him about the e-mail he had received from Carolines. He hoped that Kevin didn't suspect the message was a forgery. Several hours later, Kevin did call, and the panic was evident in his voice as he described the appeal he had received from the governor of Palau.

Kevin had evidently fallen for the joke hook, line, and sinker, but it had an unintended effect. Worn out from weeks of worrying about the weather situation on Palau, the e-mail from Carolines was the last straw for Kevin. Even though he would incur a substantial financial penalty for canceling the trip to Palau, Kevin said he had called his travel agent and told him the trip was off. He had no intention of having his dream vacation ruined by a typhoon and he wasn't about to spend his precious two weeks running rescue operations for the governor.

Not anticipating that Kevin would cancel the entire trip on account of the e-mail message, Kevin's friend immediately began having heart palpitations. He immediately blurted out that the e-mail was a hoax, hoping that Kevin was just joking around. Fortunately, although Kevin had indeed made a call to his travel agent to discuss calling off the trip, it hadn't been officially canceled yet.

The two had a good laugh over the joke, but Kevin had been seriously thinking of canceling the trip anyway. A few days later, he decided the weather situation in Palau was too much of a risk, and he decided to take his wife to the beautiful Cook Islands instead. This time, Kevin was in no hurry to tell his friend where they were going to be staying.

Source: Kevin Hendershot

ffending your customers is never good for business. Unfortunately, a reality of today's information age is that you can offend customers faster than ever before. As San Diego–based Networld Solutions knows all too well, all it takes is one small slip of the keyboard and you can offend your entire client base in under sixty seconds.

A GUARANTEED WAY TO "LOSE" BUSINESS

Networld Solutions, January 2001

The mishap arose after Networld hired a company to invite current and prospective customers to a seminar. The invitation was to go out by e-mail and Networld was hoping for a favorable response rate.

What happened next is truly hard to believe. The invitations were indeed distributed by e-mail, but the words "You are a loser" somehow appeared in the subject line of each invitation.

Recipients of the e-mail were obviously stunned. According to a *San Diego Union-Tribune* report, many of them fired back missives to Networld expressing their disgust at the message they had just received. "Is this the normal way that you address your e-mail to consultants? . . . I find this insulting to say the least," wrote one steamed customer. Another person responded, "I don't think so. But I guarantee that you won't get any business from us."

Not only did Networld have to call off their planned seminar, the company reportedly lost $75,000 as a result of the mishap. Very few customers, it seems, appreciated the lighter side of the mishap.

The goof was allegedly caused by International Data Group, a multi-national publisher and event organizer that Networld had hired to do their e-mail marketing. According to a lawsuit that Networld filed against IDG, the damaging e-mail was sent out during a training session. The lawsuit was later settled and Networld says it received compensation from IDG for the blunder.

In an interview with the *San Diego Union-Tribune*, Aaron Benedict, Networld's marketing manager, said that aside from apologizing to its customers, there wasn't much else the company could do. He offered a sobering reminder to any other organization that happens to find itself in a similar predicament: "Once an e-mail is out there, you can't get it back," he said.

Sources: Networld Solutions, *San Diego Union-Tribune*

f you want to make a company sweat, Jonah Peretti can give you a pointer or two. In January 2001, he had Nike's public relations team in a frenzy after he cleverly mocked the company in an effort to expose their alleged use of child labor.

NEVER LET THEM SEE YOU SWEAT

Nike Corporation, January 2001

t all started in January 2001 when Jonah attempted to use Nike's Web site to order a pair of customized running shoes. Nike's revolutionary shoe-design service, which was introduced with great fanfare in 1999, allowed customers to create their own shoes complete with accent colors and a personalized ID printed on the side. The service was heralded by Nike as a new form of customer empowerment, but Jonah felt that the service completely obscured the truth. Nike's shoes were actually built by child laborers in Asia, he said, not by consumers in their dens and living rooms.

Feeling a need to personally confront Nike on the controversial subject of child labor, Jonah came up with a rather unique idea. He submitted an order for a pair of running shoes and requested that they be branded with the word "sweatshop."

"The shoe customization service was designed to associate the Nike brand with personal freedom, so my prank attempted to turn the tables by using the same service to raise awareness about the limited freedom enjoyed by Nike sweatshop workers," Jonah wrote in an on-line essay describing his encounter with the apparel giant.

Thus began a rapid exchange of e-mail messages between Jonah and Nike that would make Jonah famous and embroil Nike in an unprecedented public relations crisis.

Upon receiving Jonah's first e-mail, Nike replied with a polite e-mail saying that his order had been canceled because the word he had chosen for his personalized ID had been rejected.

From: "Personalize, NIKE iD"
To: "'Jonah H. Peretti'"
Subject: RE: Your NIKE iD order o16468000

Your NIKE iD order was cancelled for one or more of the following reasons.
1) Your Personal iD contains another party's trademark or other intellectual property.
2) Your Personal iD contains the name of an athlete or team we do not have the legal right to use.
3) Your Personal iD was left blank. Did you not want any personalization?
4) Your Personal iD contains profanity or inappropriate slang, and besides, your mother would slap us.

If you wish to reorder your NIKE iD product with a new personalization please visit us again at www.nike.com
Thank you,
NIKE iD

Jonah quickly typed up a reply and sent it to Nike. He pointed out that his personal ID didn't meet any of the objectionable criteria the company had identified in their previous e-mail message.

From: "Jonah H. Peretti"
To: "Personalize, NIKE iD"
Subject: RE: Your NIKE iD order o16468000

Greetings,

My order was canceled but my personal NIKE iD does not violate any of the criteria outlined in your message. The Personal iD on my custom ZOOM XC USA running shoes was the word "sweatshop." Sweatshop is not: 1) another's party's trademark, 2) the name of an athlete, 3) blank, or 4) profanity. I choose the iD because I wanted to remember the toil and labor of the children that made my shoes. Could you please ship them to me immediately.

Thanks and Happy New Year,
Jonah Peretti

This time, Nike replied with more specific information about what was wrong with Jonah's order.

From: "Personalize, NIKE iD"
To: "'Jonah H. Peretti'"
Subject: RE: Your NIKE iD order o16468000

Dear NIKE iD Customer,

Your NIKE iD order was cancelled because the iD you
have chosen contains, as stated in the previous e-mail correspondence, "inappropriate slang." If you wish to reorder your
NIKE iD product with a new personalization please visit us
again at www.nike.com

Thank you,
NIKE iD

Not willing to let the matter go, Jonah challenged Nike on their
categorization of the word "sweatshop" as a slang word.

From: "Jonah H. Peretti"
To: "Personalize, NIKE iD"
Subject: RE: Your NIKE iD order o16468000

Dear NIKE iD,

Thank you for your quick response to my inquiry about my
custom ZOOM XC USA running shoes. Although I commend
you for your prompt customer service, I disagree with the
claim that my personal iD was inappropriate slang. After consulting Webster's Dictionary, I discovered that "sweatshop" is
in fact part of standard English, and not slang. The word
means: "a shop or factory in which workers are employed for
long hours at low wages and under unhealthy conditions" and
its origin dates from 1892. So my personal iD does meet the
criteria detailed in your first email.

Your web site advertises that the NIKE iD program is "about freedom to choose and freedom to express who you are." I share Nike's love of freedom and personal expression. The site also says that "If you want it done right...build it yourself." I was thrilled to be able to build my own shoes, and my personal iD was offered as a small token of appreciation for the sweatshop workers poised to help me realize my vision. I hope that you will value my freedom of expression and reconsider your decision to reject my order.

Thank you,
Jonah Peretti

Nike was caught between a rock and a hard place. Since when is the word "sweatshop" a slang term? Nike again replied to Jonah, staying clear of his cleverly crafted argument about the origin of the word "sweatshop" but pointing out that they have the ultimate right to reject any order they choose.

From: "Personalize, NIKE iD"
To: "'Jonah H. Peretti'"
Subject: RE: Your NIKE iD order o16468000

Dear NIKE iD Customer,

Regarding the rules for personalization it also states on the NIKE iD web site that "Nike reserves the right to cancel any Personal iD up to 24 hours after it has been submitted." In addition it further explains:

"While we honor most personal iDs, we cannot honor every one. Some may be (or contain) others' trademarks, or the names of certain professional sports teams, athletes or celebrities that Nike does not have the right to use. Others may contain material that we consider inappropriate or simply do not want to place on our products.

Unfortunately, at times this obliges us to decline personal iDs that may otherwise seem unobjectionable. In any event, we will let you know if we decline your personal iD, and we will offer you the chance to submit another."

With these rules in mind we cannot accept your order as submitted.

If you wish to reorder your NIKE iD product with a new personalization please visit us again at www.nike.com

Thank you, NIKE iD

At this point, Jonah knew he wasn't going to get his shoes, but he couldn't resist firing off one last message to Nike.

From: "Jonah H. Peretti"
To: "Personalize, NIKE iD"
Subject: RE: Your NIKE iD order o16468000

Dear NIKE iD,

Thank you for the time and energy you have spent on my request. I have decided to order the shoes with a different iD, but I would like to make one small request. Could you please send me a color snapshot of the ten-year-old Vietnamese girl who makes my shoes?

Thanks,
Jonah Peretti

Nike never responded.

Amused by Nike's refusal to allow him to print the word "sweat-shop" on his sneakers, and motivated by a need to spread the word about the company's alleged labor abuses, Jonah forwarded the entire e-mail correspondence to twelve of his friends. Within a matter of days, news of Jonah's run-in with Nike had spread to people all over the world. Dozens of Web sites made mention of the incident, and Jonah began to receive e-mail messages from all corners of the globe.

What began as a simple e-mail to a bunch of close friends had suddenly mushroomed into an international news story. Journalists quickly got wind of the story and throughout the months of February and March, Jonah was inundated with calls from radio and television stations, newspapers, and magazines. The *San Jose Mercury News,* CBC Radio, *Time* magazine, the *Wall Street Journal, USA Today,* and the *San Francisco Chronicle* were just some of the mass media outlets that reported on the anti-Nike crusade that Jonah had inspired.

Suddenly, it seemed like everyone was talking about Jonah's story. At one point, he was receiving 500 e-mail messages a day, even marriage proposals, from people who had read about his protest against Nike. To the chagrin of Nike, one person took advantage of the momentum the story was gaining and began to sell t-shirts with the Nike swoosh and the word "sweatshop" on them.

As all of this was going on, one can only imagine the scene that was unfolding at Nike headquarters in Oregon as they tried to deal with the influx of media inquiries. They also had to contend with an avalanche of requests for shoes like the ones Jonah had tried to order. Jonah had received messages from people who told him they, too, were going to the Nike Web site and asking if they could get shoes with phrases like "child labor" printed on them.

Facing renewed questions about their labor practices, Nike was suddenly forced to defend themselves in the national media. Perhaps Jonah's ultimate achievement was when NBC flew Jonah to New York to appear on the network's popular *Today* show, where he faced off against Nike spokesperson Vada Manager in a debate moderated by Katie Couric. Nike maintained in all their interviews that the company did not employ child laborers nor did they have sweatshops, a position that many human rights activists vehemently disagree with.

Several months after it began, the firestorm of controversy around Nike eventually died down, but Jonah's experience remains one of the most memorable and successful examples of on-line activism ever. It's also a valuable lesson in how a single individual can take on a multi-million-dollar corporation and make them sweat, literally.

Sources: ABC News, *Nation,* Jonah Peretti, *San Francisco Chronicle, San Jose Mercury News, USA Today, Wall Street Journal*

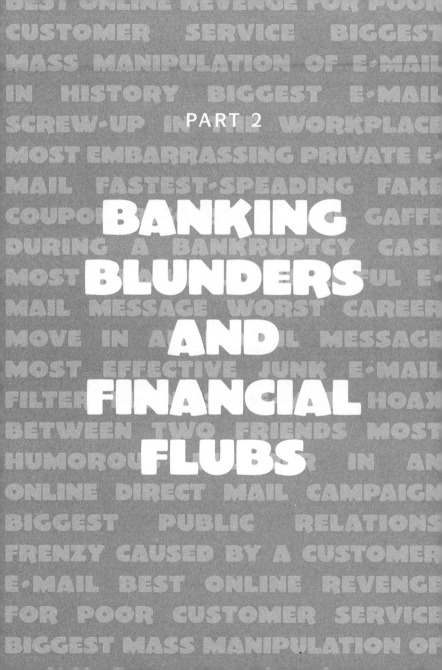

PART 2

BANKING
BLUNDERS
AND
FINANCIAL
FLUBS

It's fun to be a billionaire—even if it's just for a few minutes. Just ask Jeff Ferrera and Cindy Broadwater of Illinois. In May 1996, they used their bank's telephone banking system to get an up-to-date balance on their bank account and nearly flipped when they heard the computer tell them the total was a whopping $924,844,208.32. That put the couple just shy of being billionaires.

A BILLION-DOLLAR BOO-BOO

First National Bank of Chicago, May 1996

Jeff and Cindy weren't the only ones to receive the surprising good news. Eight hundred other customers of the bank—the First National Bank of Chicago—also received unexpected windfalls that day. Sylvester Dorsey, a bill collector for the Peoples Gas Light and Coke Company, was going out for dinner when he discovered the multimillion-dollar balance in his account after using the bank's ATM.

"I showed the receipt to a friend and we just started screaming," he said in an interview with the *Chicago Tribune*.

The bank, upon realizing that hundreds of Chicago residents were suddenly multimillionaires, immediately froze some customer accounts and began to look for the source of the massive errors. The glitch was eventually discovered and blamed on a change to a computer program.

Incredibly, the sum total of all the errors was more than *six times* the total assets of First Chicago NBD Corporation, the bank's holding company.

In an interview with the Associated Press, Ferrera said that his friends jokingly urged him to assume a new identity and wire the money to the Cayman Islands. "Nah, I couldn't run off and do that," said Ferrera, a computer technician. "It was just unique being called a billionaire for a day. It was the talk at work."

The American Bankers Association declared it the largest such error in the history of U.S. banking.

Sources: Associated Press, *Chicago Tribune*

anita McDuffy of Madison, Wisconsin, thinks she deserves a reward for her honesty, so she's holding her bank hostage for $150 million.

A LITTLE
SOMETHING FOR
HER HONESTY

First Federal Savings Bank, February 2001

er extraordinary ordeal began on February 17, 2001, when she made a routine visit to her bank to get a cashier's check for $1,500. The following Monday, she got a call from her bank, First Federal Savings, advising her that there was a small problem with the cashier's check she had been issued. Could she please come down to the bank and pick up a new check? The bank didn't specify what the problem was, so Vanita pulled out the check and examined it. That's when she noticed that the check was made out for $150,000 instead of the $1,500 she had requested. Stunned by her discovery, Vanita showed the bank's monumental goof to a relative, who had even more incredible news to deliver. Vanita had misread the amount of the check. Incredibly, the cashier's check she had in her possession was made out for a whopping $150,000,000. Yes, that's *$150 million*!

Vanita said she believed the cashier's check was cashable, at least initially, but she resisted the temptation to fly off someplace to try to capitalize on her bank's mistake. Instead, she kept the check and called a press conference to let the local media know there were still honest people left in the world. Her story made headlines across the country and caught the attention of *Good Morning America,* which flew Vanita to New York for a live, nationally televised interview with Charles Gibson.

Vanita said she could have run away with the bank's money, causing even more trouble for her financial institution. But she didn't, and Vanita has made it clear that she expects a reward for her honesty—or at the very least a sincere apology from her bank for the error.

First Federal Savings, meanwhile, has offered neither an apology nor a finder's fee to Vanita. Nor have they ever asked for the cashier's check back. As far as they're concerned, the check has been canceled and the matter is over. Vanita begs to differ. She hired a lawyer in Chicago and she's still holding on to the $150 million cashier's check, which she insists is still valid. "You can't cancel a cashier's check," she argued.

If the bank won't give her any money for the multimillion-dollar check, Vanita hopes someone else will. Realizing that she has a unique piece of financial lore in her possession, she's contemplating the possibility of auctioning it off on eBay one day.

Sources: Associated Press, Vanita McDuffy

f you noticed that there were millions of dollars of extra money in your bank account that really shouldn't be there, what would you do? Would you report your discovery to your bank or immediately make a withdrawal and see how much money you could walk away with? As the following story illustrates, sometimes it's easy to get carried away with sudden and unexpected wealth.

A BAD CASE OF WITHDRAWAL

NationsBank, May 1994

n May 1994, thirty-one-year-old Howard Jenkins of Tampa, Florida, found himself in an interesting predicament. He went to an automated teller machine to make a withdrawal and the receipt told him his bank balance was a whopping $889,437.93—just shy of a million dollars. Stunned, Jenkins went home and used the bank's telephone banking system to check his balance again. This time, he was told his balance was more than *$88 million*. Jenkins quickly went to his bank, NationsBank, and asked a teller if she could check his balance. She slid him a piece of paper with an eight-figure number on it.

Stunned at the bank's confirmation that he was indeed a multimillionaire, Jenkins almost passed out.

The teller couldn't resist asking Jenkins where the money had come from. According to the *Tampa Tribune,* she asked him, "Did you get an inheritance or something?" Not wanting to draw attention to himself, Jenkins replied, "Or something."

Jenkins decided to see how far he could press his streak of good luck. He asked the teller for $4 million. Incredibly, the bank gave it to him! (No, I am not kidding.) "They handed me $4 million and didn't bat an eye," he told the *Tribune.* Jenkins received $3,000 in cash and seven checks, one for $997,000 and six for $500,000 each.

During lunch, Jenkins showed the cash and checks to his girlfriend, who immediately told him the money had to be returned. Jenkins says he knew he had to give back the money, but he was having fun just holding the wad of cash.

Later the same day, Jenkins returned to the bank with his lawyer and turned over the money. The lawyer was present as a precaution just in case the bank tried to arrest him.

"It was a hell of a day for me," an exhilarated Jenkins told the *Tribune.* "I was a multimillionaire for about half a day."

Sources: Associated Press, *Tampa Tribune*

> f you've ever had a check bounce, you know how
> embarrassing that can be. But when eighty-four-year-old
> Helen Straub of River Park, Indiana, was informed that
> her checking account was overdrawn by almost $4
> million, it was the bank's turn to be embarrassed.

THE CHECK
THAT BOUNCED
TO THE MOON

Wells Fargo Bank, November 2002

n October 2002, Straub wrote a routine check to her local power company in the amount of $38.17. She mailed the payment, but somewhere along the line her check ballooned into a $4,000,038.17 charge against her Wells Fargo bank account.

Straub didn't have enough funds in her account to cover the gargantuan check, so the bank's computers generated a standard form letter informing Straub that her check had bounced, and instructing her to deposit $3,995,736.19 to cover the missing funds.

When Straub received the bank's correspondence in the mail, she was stunned by the bank's demands. "When I got the letter from the bank, I first thought someone had gotten in and stolen one of my checks," she told the *South Bend Tribune*.

Straub queried her bank about the strange correspondence and it was quickly determined that an error had occurred sometime during the processing of her hydro payment. Wells Fargo promptly adjusted Straub's account and waived the twenty-five-dollar fee that would normally be charged for bounced checks.

Straub, a longtime Wells Fargo customer, was happy that the problem was satisfactorily resolved, but she no doubt wished the bank had put $4 million into her account rather than taken it out.

Source: *South Bend Tribune*

aco Bell sure knows how to stir up trouble. On April Fools' Day, 1996, the fast-food chain known for their fast-talking Chihuahua took out a full-page advertisement in the *New York Times* announcing that they had purchased the Liberty Bell. Of course, it was just a joke. Six years later, the company was making headlines again, though this time through no fault of their own.

A BILL THAT'S HARD TO SWALLOW

University of Wisconsin—La Crosse, October 2002

In October 2002, some students at the University of Wisconsin in La Crosse opened their credit card statements to discover that the $3,200 tuition fee that they had charged had apparently been paid to Taco Bell.

In an interview with the local paper, the *La Crosse Tribune*, student association president Adam Mueller expressed his amusement at the gaffe. "I know some of our students eat at Taco Bell, but I never knew they racked up that big of a bill," he joked. Not sure what to make of the weird charge on their credit card bills, several students called the university to make sure their tuition had been paid in full.

An investigation by the university revealed that the glitch was caused by the company that processed the credit card payments on behalf of the university. Somehow, the company's software erroneously listed Taco Bell as the source of the charge. The university said that all the money had been correctly routed into the university's bank account, and no money had been mistakenly diverted to Taco Bell.

Nevertheless, the bizarre incident no doubt had some people speculating that Taco Bell was somehow tied to the university's bank account. Ron Lostetter, the university's vice chancellor for finance and administration, was quick to quash that rumor.

"No, Taco Bell is not part of the UW-L account," he told the *La Crosse Tribune.*

Sources: Associated Press, *La Crosse Tribune*

> heck errors are a common occurrence these days, and the reasons behind them are usually logical or at least understandable. But the excuse provided by the U.S. Agricultural Stabilization and Conservation Service for a $4 million check blunder takes the cake for the strangest explanation I've ever come across.

RANDOM ACTS OF WEIRDNESS

U.S. Agricultural Stabilization and Conservation Service,
April 1992

In April 1992, North Dakota resident Harlan Johnson was awaiting a $31 payment from the U.S. government. Johnson was a farmer in Crosby, North Dakota, and the payment was coming from a farm subsidy program that he was eligible for. But when the envelope finally arrived, Johnson was stunned to receive a check for $4,038,277.04.

Government officials became aware of the eye-popping mistake the day after the check had been mailed, and they quickly phoned Johnson and asked him to return the check as soon as he received it.

What caused this mega-blunder? Dale Ihry, who heads up the government agency's office in North Dakota, said that the $4,038,277.04 amount is a number that inexplicably shows up on agency records from time to time.

"Our computer program, for whatever reason, sometimes picks up this $4 million amount and prints it out on something," he said. "This is the first time it made it on a [check], though."

For his part, Harlan Johnson had a good laugh over the check and made a photocopy of the legendary gaffe before returning it to the government. He knew it

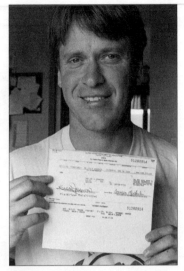

Harlan Johnson holding the $4 million check he accidentally received from the U.S. government.

was something that would probably never happen to him again.

As for the government, there was no word on whether they were going to investigate the bizarre problem or wait for the mystery $4 million number to get printed on something else.

Sources: Associated Press, *Journal* (Crosby, North Dakota), Harlan Johnson

hen Tom Spears of Ottawa, Ontario, Canada,
visited Boston, Massachusetts, on business in October
of 2002, he booked himself a standard room at a local
Holiday Inn. But looking at Tom's bill a few weeks later, you'd
think he had stayed in the presidential suite. The hotel
billed him a whopping $41,000 (U.S.) for his two-night
stay, a charge so large that it maxed out his credit card.

DECIMAL DILEMMA

Six Continents Hotels, October 2002

Tom wasn't the only one whose
credit line got zapped. Other customers of the Six Continents hotel
chain, which includes the popular Holiday Inn and Crowne Plaza brands,
also got hit with the astronomical charges as a result of a computer-
programming error at a credit-card-processing company. The snafu
resulted in tens of thousands of hotel guests being charged 100 times
more than they actually spent. Instead of charging customers a total of
$4.8 million for their hotel stays, the credit card processor mistakenly
billed them for $480 million.

CARD NUMBER -					
1	Oct. 13	Oct. 15	LAURIER OPTICAL CARLING OTTAWA ON		207.70
2	Oct. 17	Oct. 18	HO HO CHINESE FOOD OTTAWA		50.72
3	Oct. 20	Oct. 20	BLACK'S #50 OTTAWA ON		19.54
4	Oct. 20	Oct. 22	GRAND & TOY #2304 OTTAWA ON		9.19
5	Oct. 23	Oct. 25	GEMMELL'S FLOWERS, LTD. SMITHS FALLS ON		24.10
6	Oct. 24	Oct. 28	SMITHBOOKS #534 OTTAWA ON		9.62
7	Oct. 27	Oct. 28	USD41,363.00@1.597360HOLIDAY INN SELECT		66,071.60
8	Oct. 27	Oct. 29	USD41,363.00@1.596233HOLIDAY INN SELECT		66,024.99CR
9	Oct. 27	Oct. 29	USD413.63@1.596233HOLIDAY INN SELECT GVT		660.25
10	Oct. 31	Oct. 31	HOLIDAY INN SELECT-EXCHANGE DIFFERENCE		46.61CR
11	Oct. 27	Oct. 31	FX RECOVERY		46.61CR
12	Oct. 31	Oct. 31	AIR MILES 1/$40 REWARD OPTION		100CR
13	Nov. 1	Nov. 4	GRAND & TOY #2304 OTTAWA ON		45.99

The MasterCard statement received by Tom Spears, showing his $66,000 (Canadian) bill for the Holiday Inn.

This gargantuan glitch, caused by a lowly decimal point that moved two places by accident, caused chaos across North America as shoppers tried to make purchases on their credit cards, only to find out that their accounts had been suspended.

Shortly after Tom Spears returned from Boston, his wife tried to make a $30 purchase with her credit card but suffered the embarrassment of having the card declined. When she called the bank to find out why she had no credit, they told her that her husband had spent $41,363 (U.S.)—approximately $66,000 (Canadian)—at the Holiday Inn in Boston. Since the balance was way over its limit, their account had been frozen.

Betty Williams of Columbus, Ohio, ran into a similar jam while shopping at a local Wal-Mart. "I called my credit card company and they said I had an $18,000 balance," she told the Associated Press. "They said there's a $17,600 charge from the Holiday Inn, and I said, 'Wow, we only stayed one night!'"

Other hotel guests had similar horror stories, but the people who got hit the worst were those who paid for their hotel stays with debit cards. They had their bank accounts emptied by the inflated charges.

The scope of the glitch was enormous. It is estimated that about 26,000 people were affected, making it the largest billing error in the history of the hotel chain and quite possibly the largest billing mess in the history of the hotel industry. Many customers were understandably irate at the mishap, but they can take comfort in knowing it could have been much worse. Just imagine if that misbehaving decimal point had moved three places by accident rather than two. If that had happened, the overcharges would have soared to almost $5 billion!

Sources: Associated Press, *Ottawa Citizen,* Six Continents Hotels, Tom Spears, *Wall Street Journal*

When California resident Barbara Mitchell left a one-cent tip for her waiter after dining at a local restaurant, it was no accident. Mitchell thought the service was lousy and she wanted the waiter to get the message loud and clear.

TIP·SY TURVY

Costa Mesa, California, February 1998

Her meal of Caesar salad, minestrone soup, pasta, and iced tea had come to a grand total of $24.20. With a one-cent gratuity, the total bill was $24.21. But when the waiter attempted to enter Mitchell's measly $0.01 tip into the restaurant's computer, he accidentally entered 010000, which the computer read as $10,000.

Mitchell was unaware of the error until she got her credit card bill and noticed that the restaurant had billed her a whopping $10,024.21 for her unsatisfactory lunch. She immediately complained to her credit card company, which investigated the bogus charge and agreed to remove it from Mitchell's bill.

The waiter was suspended for one week because of the mistake and Mitchell was offered a gift certificate as compensation for the inflated bill. The manager of the restaurant explained that they had tried to correct the $10,000 overcharge the day after Mitchell had dined there, but their computer wouldn't allow such a big credit. So it was left on the bill and Mitchell got quite a surprise when her monthly credit card statement arrived in the mail.

Despite the minor inconvenience caused by the inflated bill, Mitchell said she found the whole incident quite amusing. "It's so ridiculous, it's funny," she told the *Orange County Register.* "I should have left cash."

Source: *Orange County Register*

When Shane Shafer of Georgetown, Texas, got his
December water bill in January 2002, it was like a
freight train heading toward his bank account.

A TITANIC·SIZED WATER BILL

City of Georgetown, Texas, January 2002

Because of a malfunction in the
city's billing system, Shafer got a bill for a whopping $21,297.33—about
$21,270 more than normal. Although he was assured he wouldn't have
to pay the ridiculous sum, that turned out to be the least of his problems.
Because Shafer used the city's automatic debit system, the amount of
the bill was scheduled to be deducted from his account within a few
days. But he didn't have enough money in his account to cover the huge
withdrawal, and the transaction was going to wipe out his savings. With
no money left in his account, Shafer was worried that his checks would
begin bouncing, which would in turn affect his credit rating.

Shafer complained to the city, and to his astonishment, they told
him there was absolutely nothing they could do to stop the automated

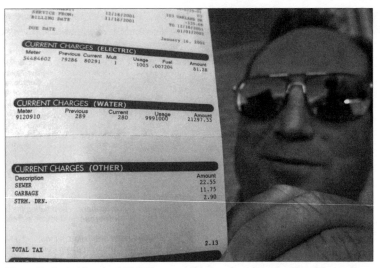

Shane Shafer holding the $21,000 water bill he received from the City of Georgetown.

debit. A financial train wreck was coming and there was no way to reverse it.

The city came up with a quick solution and planned to send Shafer a $21,000 check to cover the automated withdrawal. In the end, however, the crisis was averted when Shane's bank managed to find a way to stop the money from being taken from his bank account.

The billing error that affected Shafer also affected fourteen other homes on the same utility route, but Shane was the only one of the fifteen homes that was using automated debit.

"I didn't realize how vulnerable my cash assets were," Shafer told the *Austin American-Statesman*. He told the paper that he's going to stick to writing checks from now on.

Source: *Austin American-Statesman*

EXCUSE FOR SPENDING SOMEONE ELSE'S MONEY

If you worked at a bank and a couple approached
you wondering how $251,197 had suddenly appeared
in their near-empty bank account, what would you do?
Investigate, or tell the couple the money must have
come from an anonymous donor?

251,197 REASONS
TO THANK GOD

Delaware, Ohio, September 1997

Believe it or not, a bank in Delaware,
Ohio, ran into this exact situation and they actually told the couple to
keep the money. It's one of the strangest reactions from a bank I've ever
come across.

This bizarre incident happened to John and Patricia Foote of
Delaware, Ohio, in 1997. On September 29 of that year, they discovered
that over a quarter-million dollars had inexplicably appeared in their
business account with Huntington National Bank. The religious couple
repeatedly questioned their bank about where the large sum of money
had come from, and they repeatedly got assurances from Huntington

that the money was theirs to keep. Even though the couple's account previously had a balance of only $402, the bank seemed satisfied that the couple's sudden windfall was not a mistake.

The Footes were uncomfortable not knowing where their good fortune had come from, so they asked the bank for the donor's name, explaining that they wanted to thank the mystery philanthropist for his or her generosity. According to Mr. Foote, who spoke to the *Columbus Dispatch,* the bank replied, "When they want you to know, they'll tell you."

With no evidence to the contrary, the couple concluded that God must have given them the money and they proceeded to spend it. They donated $130,000 to a number of Christian ministries and bought $84,000 worth of vehicles and trailers, which were used to help build churches along the East Coast. They also used some of the money in their own missionary work. "We thought God had somehow given us that money," Mr. Foote told the *Columbus Dispatch.*

But the Footes' wild spending spree had a surprise ending. Federal authorities sued their company for bank fraud after it was discovered the money wasn't theirs to spend. It turned out that the money actually belonged to someone else and it had been placed in the Footes' bank account as a result of a clerical error. But the goof wasn't discovered until 18 months later, and by that time, almost all the money was gone.

A U.S. district court judge ordered the Footes' company to repay all the money to Huntington National Bank, but the company went bankrupt, and the bank was unable to recover the funds.

"You can't get money out of a dead company," said the couple's lawyer. He said the federal authorities decided against charging the couple with bank fraud because they realized it would be difficult to prove criminal intent. "After all, they used most of [the money] for religious work. The government would have had a tough time convincing a jury that these people are criminals," he said.

No doubt the Footes are thanking God for that!

Source: *Columbus Dispatch*

In November 1998, a scene reminiscent of the classic 1983 movie *WarGames* played out across Europe.

WELCOME TO THE REAL WORLD

London, England, November 1998

The now-famous incident took place in London, England, where a junior trader at a German financial institution was fiddling around with a computer-simulated training program. Like Matthew Broderick's character in *WarGames,* the trader thought he was doing a simulation, but he got the shock of his life when he realized that the mock trades had actually been executed on Eurex, a German-based electronic exchange that is used for trading German bond futures.

To make matters worse, the trades he had mistakenly authorized were worth around *$19 billion* (U.S.). *The Guardian* described the gaffe as "probably the biggest blunder ever witnessed in modern markets."

Panic ensued on the trading floor as traders were alerted to the news that someone wanted to sell 130,000 German bond-futures contracts with a value of more than $19 billion.

"It was absolutely extraordinary," said one London futures trader quoted by *The Guardian*. "We were all gathered around the screen and everyone was just looking in disbelief. Then we hit the phones."

Another trader expressed similar disbelief at what he saw on his computer screen. "At first I thought this was a Rio trade, which is where someone makes a last-ditch attempt to recover losses by betting their bank or, if that fails, books a one-way ticket to Brazil."

Although many traders knew right away that the massive sell order had to be a catastrophic mistake, they cashed in anyway and began buying the futures contracts that had been mistakenly put on the market. Deutsche Terminbörse (DTB), the German options and futures exchange, which is a partner in Eurex, eventually ruled that the original sell offers would stand, and the German bank that employed the careless trader was forced to buy back the contracts at higher prices. The total cost to the German bank was estimated to have been about $16 million (U.S.).

According to people familiar with the Eurex trading system, the trader's slipup was understandable because the training program and the actual trading system look nearly identical. But that is likely of little consolation to this unlucky junior trader, whose employer had to foot an enormous bill because of his unprecedented mistake.

Sources: Associated Press, *Guardian, London Daily Telegraph,* Reuters

> f you think the president of the United States has a lot of power at his fingertips, just look at what a stockbroker can do.

BUTTER FINGERS

Lehman Brothers, May 2001

n May 2001, a Lehman Brothers trader in London was keying in a transaction involving the shares of companies in the Financial Times Stock Exchange 100 Index, when he accidentally added two zeros to the sell order.

It sounds innocent enough, but the trader's mistake was colossal. Instead of trading 3 million pounds' worth of shares, he generated a sell order worth an astonishing *300 million pounds*. This inadvertent trade stripped 30 billion pounds off the market value of Britain's largest companies and sent the Financial Times Index tumbling around 130 points and several percentage points. The trade came at the very end of the trading day and sent shock waves through the market as brokers watched their computer screens in disbelief.

The good news was that the trade involved the firm's own money, so Lehman's clients didn't lose any money of their own. But the poor trader was believed to have cost his own employer at least 6 million pounds. And as if that wasn't punishment enough, the London Stock Exchange fined the investment bank an additional 20,000 pounds for the error. Although many people expected that the employee would be sacked over the incident, Lehman Brothers allowed the unlucky trader to keep his job.

Said one dealer quoted by the *Independent* newspaper, "This is every trader's nightmare. You pray it won't happen to you."

Sources: *Daily Mail, Guardian, Independent, Sunday Telegraph*

TRADING BLUNDER ON THE NEW YORK STOCK EXCHANGE

The *Wall Street Journal* called it "unthinkable" and the equivalent of a "nuclear disaster." A New York trader described it as a "misguided missile." The *Seattle Times* labeled it "the biggest bungle of all time." And it remains the most talked-about trading mistake in the history of the New York Stock Exchange.

PANIC ON WALL STREET

Salomon Brothers, March 1992

At 3:55 P.M. on March 26, 1992, a clerk working for Salomon Brothers in New York misread a trading order and mistakenly sold 11 million *shares of stock* instead of $11 million *worth of stock*. It was estimated that as much as $500 million worth of stock was mistakenly dumped on the New York Stock Exchange that day, just moments before the closing bell, causing near pandemonium on the trading floor.

According to Salomon Brothers, one of their big customers submitted an order to sell $11 million worth of different stocks. However, when the clerk processed the order, he accidentally typed "11 million" in the area on his computer screen where the number of shares was to be specified.

The 11 million shares of stock were estimated to be worth as much as $500 million, obviously a much bigger dollar amount than the $11 million in stocks that the clerk was supposed to sell, so the impact was massive and immediate.

Within minutes of the erroneous trade's being executed, the selling pressure caused the Dow Jones Industrial Average to take a nosedive, plunging around 16 points, and some of America's largest companies saw millions wiped off their market value. Quaker Oats lost a whopping $125 million, Xerox stock plunged by nearly $50 million, and nearly $16 million vanished off the market value of Motorola.

People who witnessed the panic on the trading floor said they saw Michael Crooks, one of Salomon's trading managers, in a shouting match with another senior trader as Crooks tried to buy stock futures in an attempt to curtail the company's losses.

Salomon said they were able to stop part of the order from going through but not all of it. This was certainly good news for the Salomon employee who made the huge mistake. He was never identified by name, but he got to keep his job and was never disciplined for the accidental trade. Salomon called it an "innocent mistake."

Innocent or not, the story made headlines around the world and sparked intense debate about how to prevent similar botched trades in the future. One of the best comments came from a former Salomon employee quoted in the *Wall Street Journal*:

"What concerns me," he said, "is what happens when we go to these wonderful twenty-first-century trading systems and somebody makes this kind of mistake at three o'clock in the morning, and you and I wake up and the market is down 275 points."

Sources: *Seattle Times, Wall Street Journal*

In 1998, a Salomon Smith Barney trader in London was embroiled in an embarrassing incident that saw him succumb to the first ever severe case of "trader's elbow."

WHAT YOU DON'T KNOW ABOUT YOUR COMPUTER CAN HURT YOU

Salomon Smith Barney, July 1998

The trader was at his desk on July 23, 1998, when he inadvertently leaned on a key on his computer and accidentally sold 14,500 French government-bond contracts worth a staggering $1.3 billion. The unintentional transaction on Matif, the French futures exchange, stood out like a molehill in a flat desert because it was worth more than 10 percent of the average daily volume on the exchange at the time. The sell order took everyone by surprise and shattered what had otherwise been an uneventful trading day.

"It was a quiet day," said Jacob Long, a trader at Banque Nationale de Paris, in an interview with Bloomberg News. Long had just returned to his desk after venturing out to get a quick snack, when all hell broke loose. "I was just starting to eat and suddenly the ten-year [bond] just plummets," he explained.

The sell pressure caused the price of bond contracts to fall by 1.4 percent in just a few

On July 23, 1998, a trader's elbow caused a $1.3 billion transaction to be executed by accident.

minutes. A number of banks quickly swooped in and picked up just over 10,000 of the contracts at the lower prices, leaving Salomon with a multimillion-dollar loss. Although Salomon immediately canceled the sales that didn't go through, they were unable to convince the French futures exchange to void all the trades. Salomon was stunned, as was the French futures exchange, which said an accident of this magnitude had never happened before.

It turned out that the trader had inadvertently leaned on a special "instant sell" button on his keyboard that repeated the last trade executed by the computer. To make matters worse, he leaned on the button so long that the trade was repeated an astonishing 145 times!

So why wasn't the trader more cautious? Salomon said that the "instant sell" button wasn't covered in the training course provided to traders, nor was it mentioned in the training manual, so most traders didn't even know the powerful button existed.

Sources: Bloomberg News, *Houston Chronicle, Wall Street Journal*

itibank apparently wanted to make sure Dallas Hill Jr. got their message loud and clear, so they rejected his credit card application to AT&T Universal Card Services almost 3,000 times. Yes, that's *3,000* times.

"HOW MANY TIMES DO I HAVE TO SAY NO?"

Citibank, March 2002

In March 2002, a mail carrier attempted to deliver 2,986 rejection letters from Citibank to Hill's home in Telford, Tennessee, but he wasn't in, so the mail carrier left him a note and hauled the massive delivery back to the Telford Post Office.

Hill went by the post office to see the mountain of mail and was no doubt astonished by the stack of identical letters. Each letter bore the same delivery address, the same return address, and the same message inside. "Dear Dallas Hill," the letter read, "we regret we are unable to approve your application. We can accept only one application for the same solicitation, and you have already responded to our offer."

Hill's father, Dallas Hill Sr., had recently applied for a credit card from AT&T Universal as well. Since Dallas Hill Jr. had the same name as his father, Citibank's computers mistakenly rejected his application because they thought he had already applied for the card. A subsequent computer glitch then caused the rejection notice to be issued again and again—2,986 times, to be exact.

Telford, Tennessee, is a small town of approximately 1,200 people, so the 2,986 letters overwhelmed the tiny community's post office. In fact, there were more letters for Dallas Hill Jr. than there were people in the entire town!

Bob Purgason, Telford's postmaster, said that he had never seen anything like it in his twenty-seven years with the United States Postal Service. "I've never seen that many letters from one company to one individual at one time," he told the *Johnson City Press.*

As for Dallas Hill Jr., there was no problem with his credit (or his father's, for that matter) and he ended up getting his credit card after all, along with some compensation from AT&T for the inconvenience and embarrassment caused by their unusual computer error.

Sources: Citibank, Dallas Hill Sr., *Johnson City Press,* Bob Purgason

> t must have looked like a scene straight out of Las Vegas.

A HUGE CHIP OFF THE H&R BLOCK

H&R Block, February 2002

When a Philadelphia couple went to a local H&R Block office to cash their tax-refund check in February 2002, the cash machine went nuts and began spitting out tens of thousands of dollars—much more than the $2,250 refund they had been expecting. Like water in an overflowing toilet, money continued to gush out of the machine, leaving both husband and wife in a state of disbelief.

The couple knew something was terribly wrong, but they let the excitement of the moment get the better of them. According to witnesses who saw the incident take place, the would-be thieves scooped up a heap of cash and fled the scene.

Meanwhile, an employee of H&R Block became aware of the hemorrhaging machine and tried to stop it from dispensing cash. The power was shut off, but not before a total of $72,000 had flown out of the device.

Over the next few hours, the daring couple went on a wild spending spree, splurging on beer, champagne, and cash gifts for their friends. They reportedly stashed the remaining money under a mattress and their basement staircase.

A manhunt was launched for the husband-and-wife duo, but the two thieves quickly turned themselves in once they realized the police were after them. The couple claimed they had spent only about $700 during their shopping fling, and they handed over the balance of the money in their possession—approximately $14,300—to the police.

So where was the rest of the money? The H&R Block employee who arrived on the scene that day was able to grab $37,500 of the money before anyone else took it. That left almost $20,000 still unaccounted for. The couple's lawyers said other customers or H&R Block employees might have escaped with the cash, but the prosecutors didn't buy that explanation, and both husband and wife were charged with theft and conspiracy.

As for the cash dispenser–turned–slot machine, it turned out that a clerk thousands of miles away in Texas was responsible for the blunder. When the couple inserted their $2,250 refund check, the clerk operating the remote-controlled machine accidentally authorized a payment of $225,000 rather than $2,250. The machine held a total of $100,000, and $72,000 poured out before the power was cut off.

Ironically, the same week the couple made off with their cash bonanza, a man managed to distract employees at the same H&R Block office and steal more than $950,000 in refund checks.

In an interview with the *Philadelphia Inquirer*, a police official joked that the branch's streak of bad luck might be too much for the company to handle. "I don't think the H&R Block at Fortieth and Market is going to be in business too much longer," he remarked, "because I don't think Mr. Bloch is going to like losing so much."

Sources: Associated Press, *Philadelphia Inquirer*

If you've ever been granted a loan by your bank, you know that receiving your monthly statement in the mail is a rather sobering affair. It's a depressing reminder of how much money the bank is raking in at your expense. Obviously, it's hard to find much humor in that.

HUMOR YOU CAN BANK ON

Wells Fargo Bank, February 1988

But in February 1988, thousands of home-equity-loan customers of Wells Fargo Bank got a bit of unexpected levity on their monthly statements.

At the bottom of the statement, there was usually a short marketing message promoting a new bank product or informing customers about the latest interest rate. But the February statement contained this stunning paragraph:

You owe your soul to the company store; why not owe your home to Wells Fargo? An equity advantage account can help you spend what would have been your children's inheritance.

While some customers no doubt had a good laugh at this bit of bank humor, other customers, needless to say, were aghast, and Wells Fargo's switchboard lit up like a Christmas tree. Embarrassed bank officials immediately launched an investigation to find out how such a message could have found its way onto their official account statements.

It turned out the bank had decided not to put a blurb on the February statement, but somehow the bank's computer picked up a message that had been written as an inside joke. One of the computer programmers at the bank had apparently created the humorous message during a test and it wound up getting printed on the actual bank statements.

"Instead of writing something like 'Mary had a little lamb,' they wrote that," Kim Kellogg, a bank spokeswoman, said in an interview with the *Orange County Register.* "Obviously, it does not convey the opinions of the bank and its employees."

Incredibly, no one at the bank or at the company doing the mailing caught the egregious blunder before the statements were mailed. The message also escaped the bank's normal approval process.

On February 11, a red-faced executive at the bank wrote a letter of apology to the customers who had received the statements.

"I wish to extend my personal apology for a message printed on your EquityLine statement dated February 2, 1988," the letter read. "This message was not a legitimate one. It was developed as part of a test program by a staff member, whose sense of humor was somewhat misplaced, and it was inadvertently inserted in that day's statement mailing. The message in no way conveys the opinion of Wells Fargo Bank or its employees."

What did the bank learn from this unfortunate, yet humorous, incident? "From now on, we're just going to type 'Testing One, Two, Three' at the bottom," said Kellogg in an interview with the *Washington Post*.

Sources: *Orange County Register, Washington Post*

PART 3

BUSINESS BLOOPERS, HIGH-TECH HOAXES, AND MEDICAL MIRACLES

I suppose it was only a matter of time before modern technology caught up with Superman. And in 1998, it finally happened. In August of that year, a popular Japanese men's magazine reported that Sony had inadvertently developed a camera with X-ray vision—a special power that has long been the exclusive purview of superheroes like Superman.

A CAMERA
WITH INDECENT
EXPOSURE

Sony Corporation, August 1998

In a shocking article, the Japanese publication *Takarajima* revealed that some of Sony's Handycam camcorders could be easily modified to allow them to see through people's clothes in the daytime. According to the magazine, the glitch affected Sony camcorders equipped with the NightShot utility—a special feature that makes it possible to film in the dark.

The Japanese researchers discovered that if you took a Sony Handycam equipped with the night-vision capability and placed an inexpensive filter over the lens during the daytime, you could sometimes see beneath swimsuits and other items of clothing when the night-vision feature was turned on.

As you might expect, Sony executives were appalled by the discovery. "We never imagined such a use would be possible," said Sony spokesperson Hiroaki Komatsu, according to the Associated Press. Sony immediately halted further shipments of the cameras and began modifying them to block their covert capabilities.

As word leaked out about the see-through camera, camera stores began receiving calls from anxious consumers interested in getting their hands on one. "I've sold half a dozen this morning alone. One guy came in and bought two of them," said Steve White, general manager of an Arlington, Virginia–based camera store, who was quoted by the Associated Press at the time.

Some experts were quick to point out that the effectiveness of the see-through capability was somewhat limited. But Sony, which wasted no time in doing its own tests, reported that the camera did indeed have the power to see beyond clothes under certain conditions.

"Engineers in Japan tried to replicate what was done in the news story," Sony spokesperson Dulcie Neiman explained to the *Washington Post.* "In some very special circumstances—depending on the daylight, the type of clothing, the texture, the color, the thickness, how much clothing is worn, the distance of the person to the camera—that reported capability could be replicated."

Sony has tried to put this embarrassing episode behind them, but the superhuman cameras remain for sale on the Internet, a reminder of one of the most amusing product blunders in modern business history.

Sources: Associated Press, *Washington Post*

> It seems that modern computers burn more than just CDs these days.

THE HEAT IS ON

Stockholm, Sweden, September 2002

While working at home one day in 2002, a Swedish scientist accidentally burned his genitals as he was using a laptop computer.

According to a graphic description of the incident in Britain's *The Lancet* medical journal, the unidentified scientist had placed the computer on his lap and had been writing a report for about an hour when he started feeling a burning sensation in his groin area.

The area became red and inflamed the following day, and blisters appeared on both his penis and his scrotal skin.

But the worst was yet to come. A few days later, the painful blisters broke and became infected, and pus began to seep from the wounds. Healing began to occur more than a week later, but not before "dry crusts" had formed on the infected areas.

You're probably wondering why the hapless scientist wasn't wearing pants. Well, the amazing part of this story is that the scientist *was* fully clothed—he was wearing both trousers and underpants.

Ironically, his computer manual did contain a warning about the hazards of placing the device on one's skin:

Do not allow your portable computer to operate with the base resting directly on exposed skin. With extended operation, heat can potentially build up in the base. Allowing sustained contact with the skin could cause discomfort or, eventually, a burn.

But who would have thought the heat generated by a computer could burn right through a person's clothes? The doctor who reported the incident, Claes-Goran Ostenson of the Karolinska Institute in Sweden, said the poor scientist's ordeal should be a warning to other laptop users: This story "should be taken as a serious warning against use of a laptop in a literal sense," he said.

Sources: Agence France-Presse, Karolinska Institute, *Lancet, Register,* Reuters

> For a few days in March 2001, the Hilton Hotel at
> Mexico City International Airport became one of the most
> talked about hotels in the Hilton chain. And it wasn't the
> hotel's French chef that everyone was raving about—it
> was the hotel's unbelievably low rates.

ZERO SUM GAME

Hilton Hotels, March 2001

A sharp-eyed customer of
Travelocity.com, an on-line travel-booking service, happened to be
checking out the hotel one day when he noticed that rooms were being
offered for a nightly rate of zero dollars. Eager to share the news of his
incredible discovery with other bargain hunters, he posted the following
message on FlyerTalk.com, an on-line bulletin board for travelers:

> **Just a few moments ago, I was browsing/shopping for hotels
> in the travelocity.com Web site. I was extremely surprised
> to see that the Hilton Mexico is offering $0 per night along
> with some $130 per night rooms during the month of August.**

I immediately click "Book Now" to see if it works and it did! I have 4 pages of detaily (sic) and clearly written confirmation (Hilton's confirmation # + Travelocity's reservation #) confirming a rate of $0 for two with a King size bed standard room. I also have an e-mail confirmation which states the exact same thing. This is incredible. I am pretty sure it's another computer glitch, but hey, it's not my fault and it's perfectly legal. Just thought you guys might want to check that out yourselves. Go to www.travelocity.com and see for yourself. It may still be available."

Word of Hilton's computer glitch quickly spread through the on-line travel community, and excited travelers began snapping up rooms at the Mexico City hotel like they were going out of style. "Thanks for the tip! I booked 29 nights in July," wrote one traveler. "Thank you, this will allow me to achieve diamond status. I have booked 12 stays in August at $0 per stay," beamed another. One user boasted that he had booked 90 nights at the hotel. "Let the games begin," he wrote.

As they entertained the possibility that their free rooms would actually be honored, numerous users began fantasizing about the reward points they were going to earn with their complimentary stays. Others hatched elaborate plans to get their loyalty points without actually having to stay at the hotel. "Maybe I'll fly down, check in, fly home. Then fly back and check out at the end of the month... Or I could probably check out over the phone," schemed one user.

Curious as to whether the zero-dollar rate was too good to be true, several of the travelers who had scooped up rooms at the hotel began calling Hilton to confirm their free stays. Incredibly, most of the travelers received both verbal and written confirmation of their reservations. "I have just spoken to a Hilton rep and she confirmed my dates and the rate. I also have a fax from Hilton confirming said reservation. I don't think it will be possible for them to weasel out," wrote one traveler on FlyerTalk.

But Hilton did indeed weasel out several days later, scuttling the dreams of dozens of travelers and possibly putting an end to one user's impromptu wedding plans in Mexico City. According to the hotel chain, eighty reservations were made at the zero rate, which had appeared on Hilton's own Web site as well as on other Web-based travel services. Hilton stated that it wasn't going to honor the free rooms because they were obviously posted in error. Indeed, an investigation revealed that the free-for-all occurred as a result of an oversight at the chain's Mexico City property. "We had people booking 10, 15, even 30 nights. This is an airport property; the average length of a stay is 1.1 nights," the hotel's sales director told the *Wall Street Journal.*

In the end, however, each affected customer did get something for nothing. As a gesture of goodwill, Hilton offered each person a free night's stay at the hotel.

Sources: FlyerTalk.com, *Wall Street Journal*

A Canadian woman got an unexpected surprise from a metal detector in her city's airport—a clue about the source of her persistent stomach cramps.

A GUT-WRENCHING ORDEAL

Regina, Saskatchewan, Canada, October 2002

The unidentified woman was preparing to fly from Regina, Saskatchewan, to Calgary, Alberta, in October 2002, but she was stopped at the airport's security checkpoint when the metal detector went off. The woman was searched for metal objects, but none could be found, and she was allowed to continue on her way. Puzzled airport security guards were no doubt at a loss to explain why the machine kept beeping every time the woman passed through it.

The woman had been suffering from stomach pain ever since she had undergone abdominal surgery four months earlier, and doctors had been unable to diagnose the problem. But after witnessing the mysterious behavior of the airport metal detector, the woman took herself to a medical clinic and asked for an X-ray.

Lo and behold, the X-ray showed that the woman had an 11.7-inch-long surgical retractor inside her abdomen—the type of instrument that surgeons use to hold incisions open. It was apparently left inside her body by accident during the operation. Doctors were flabbergasted by the discovery.

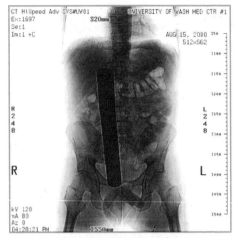

A CT scan of a man in Washington State who had a retractor accidentally left in his stomach following major abdominal surgery. The retractor was discovered by the man's physician, who noticed an odd bulge in his patient's stomach.

"I've been in this job for sixteen years and I don't think I've ever heard of an instrument of this size being left in," said Dr. Dennis Kendel, registrar for Saskatchewan's College of Physicians and Surgeons, according to the Canadian Press.

The woman's lawyer, Jeff Scott, said his client was stunned that she had been walking around with a large surgical instrument in her stomach for four months. "I would think that it would be an understatement to say [it was a] surprise, probably more like a horror, that this surgical device was left inside her abdominal cavity," he told the Canadian Broadcasting Corporation (CBC).

Despite the fact that all surgical instruments are supposed to be accounted for both before and after surgery, somehow the retractor got left behind. "Systems are never perfect and, as always, we strive to do the best we can. But inevitably, in any system, there tends to be the occasional failure," said Brian Laursen, senior vice president of the Regina Health Authority, in an interview with the CBC.

The day after the X-ray was taken, the woman was wheeled into surgery for a second time and the retractor was removed from her belly. The hospital and surgeon are now facing a potential lawsuit from the patient, who says she wants compensation for the accident.

As miraculous as this incident may seem, this isn't the first time that such a medical mistake has occurred. In 2000, a man in Washington State discovered that a retractor had been left in his stomach following major abdominal surgery. The misplaced surgical tool was eventually discovered by the man's family doctor, but not before the man had endured more than two months of excruciating pain. "Figure out how you would wear a ruler inside you and add an inch," he told the *Seattle Post-Intelligencer.*

Surgeons had dismissed the man's symptoms as typical post-operative pain, but his family doctor noticed an "oddly shaped lump" in the patient's stomach during an examination. A CT scan was ordered and that's when the retractor was discovered.

To compensate the man for the ordeal, the University of Washington Medical Center paid him a settlement of nearly $100,000. Ralph Brindley, the man's attorney, said the eye-popping error was egregious. "It was a mistake the equivalent of missing a tow truck parked on your front lawn," he told the *Seattle Post-Intelligencer.*

The man said he was grateful to be alive, but he said if he ever had to undergo surgery again, he wanted the entire procedure to be videotaped—just to be safe.

Sources: BBC News, Canadian Broadcasting Corporation, Canadian Press, Firmani & Associates, *Seattle Post-Intelligencer*

Hoaxes have become a fact of life on the Internet. But rarely do they cause the types of devastating financial losses that were experienced by Emulex Corporation, a California-based hardware and software manufacturer, on Friday, August 25, 2000.

HOW NOT TO EMUL·ATE A PRESS RELEASE

Emulex, August 2000

At 9:30 EDT that morning, just as the financial markets opened for trading, a press release, formatted to look like it came from Emulex, was posted on Internet Wire, one of the lesser-known services for news releases.

The press release announced that Emulex's president and chief executive officer, Paul Folino, had resigned, that the U.S. Securities and Exchange Commission (SEC) was conducting a formal investigation of accounting irregularities at the company, and that the company's fourth-quarter earnings would be restated to reflect losses.

Emulex's stock had closed the prior evening at $113.06, but shortly after the news release was issued, the stock began its downward spiral. By 10:13 A.M. EDT, it was trading at around $103, a 10 percent drop in its value.

News of the stunning announcement soon reached major wire services across the United States. Needless to say, the news business is intensely competitive and the financial wires take great pride in beating their competitors to the wire with a major story.

Bloomberg News was the first out of the gate. At 10:13 and 10:14 EDT that morning, Bloomberg released headlines reporting that Emulex was under investigation by the U.S. government and that the company planned to restate its fourth-quarter earnings. The headlines immediately appeared on trading desks throughout Wall Street.

A few minutes later, word of Emulex's troubles began to spread on Internet message boards.

Investors, upon hearing the shocking news, began unloading their Emulex shares. Within minutes of Bloomberg's reports hitting the wire, the shares plunged another $10 and approached $90. At 10:20 A.M., the stock fell to $75. By 10:26 A.M., it was down to near $50. With the stock in a virtual free all, millions of dollars began to vanish from pension funds, retirement accounts and people's personal savings. Incredibly, with each $10 drop in the stock price, investors collectively lost a whopping $360 million.

While all of this was going on, employees were beginning to arrive at Emulex's West Coast head office, unaware of the crisis unfolding in New York.

Kirk Roller, Emulex's senior vice president, was given the shocking news as soon as he walked in the door. "I walked in, my administrative assistant immediately said to me, 'The stock's down 45 points,'" he told the *New York Times*. "By the time I got to Paul, the stock was down 68."

Horror stories were recounted by many Emulex shareholders. "One victim I talked to purchased the stocks for $108 a share, went to the bathroom, and when he came back, they were worth $60 a share," said Paul Bertrand, a special agent from the FBI's Securities Fraud Squad, in an interview with the *B.U. Bridge,* a Boston University community newspaper.

At Emulex's corporate headquarters in California, Roller and Folino huddled together and scoured the company's recent press releases to try to identify what could be causing the stock's horrific free fall. At around 10:25 A.M., a call came in from an Emulex salesperson in Washington who said he had found an "Emulex" press release on the Internet. He immediately faxed the suspect release to Roller and Folino, and it became apparent to the two executives that the company had been the target of an elaborate scam.

It was at that point that Emulex asked the National Association of Securities Dealers (NASD) to halt trading in the company's stock, which NASD did at 10:29 A.M. EDT. By that time, Emulex shares had plunged to about $45.

In just fifteen minutes, the company's stock had plummeted from $103 to $45, wiping more than $2 billion from the company's market valuation. The panic had the effect of pulling down the entire NASDAQ stock market.

During the next twenty-five minutes, the false rumors continued to circulate. Around 10:40 A.M., Dow Jones Newswires released a headline about Emulex's fourth-quarter loss, further adding to investor confusion.

About twenty minutes later, Dow Jones learned they had been duped and they quickly issued a story to set the record straight. Bloomberg and CNBC followed with their own stories about the hoax.

At 12:51 P.M., after conferring with the FBI, SEC investigators, and some of its largest investors, Emulex issued a press release categorically

denying the information contained in the earlier news release. "The negative statements in this fictitious press release are categorically false,"
Emulex's president said in the release. "Emulex shareholders should be
assured that our business is at record levels and the fundamentals of our
business and my commitment to this company have never been stronger."

Fortunately, the company had the rest of the trading day to recoup
its devastating financial losses. Once trading resumed early in the afternoon and investors learned that the press release had been a hoax,
Emulex stock began to climb again.

At the end of the day, the shares closed at $105.75, or down 6.5
percent for the day, in trading of 11.2 million shares, more than five
times the average. The U.S. Securities and Exchange Commission believed
investors lost about $110 million as a result of the prank and the stock's
subsequent roller-coaster ride. Bloomberg said it was the first time in
their history that they had been the victim of such a prank.

It didn't take long for the FBI to track down the person responsible
for this eye-popping crime. It turned out that the culprit was Mark
Jakob, a former employee of Internet Wire, the wire service that had
carried the phony news release.

As a former employee, Jakob knew the workings of Internet Wire's
system, and this inside information helped him to perpetrate the fraud.
He made up a name—Ross Porter—and pretended he was with Emulex's
public relations firm. He then sent an e-mail under that name to Internet
Wire's nighttime staff, along with the phony press release. The e-mail
contained language that only customers of Internet Wire would know,
so staff there were fooled into thinking the press release was real.

Jakob decided to pull the prank after he got himself into debt playing
the stock market. He tried to sell Emulex stock short, but his plan
backfired and he found himself facing a potential loss of $97,000. In an
effort to recoup his losses, he made up a phony Emulex press release

that stated that the company was being forced to restate its earnings. When the stock plunged, Jakob was able to recover his losses and sell the stock at a profit.

Federal investigators apprehended Jakob on August 31, less than a week after the hoax began, and charged him with securities and wire fraud. In making the arrest, the government called Jakob's prank "one of the most devastating financial hoaxes committed in the Internet Age."

In a settlement reached with the U.S. government, Jakob agreed to pay a total fine of more than $440,642, which included the $241,000 profit he made trading Emulex stock, the $97,000 loss he tried to avoid by concocting the hoax, interest payments, and a civil penalty of $102,642. He was also sentenced to nearly four years in prison.

What lesson can be learned from the Emulex hoax? Perhaps the *Online Journalism Review* said it best: "If there's anything to be gleaned from the saga of the Emulex hoax, it's that sometimes, even in these highly competitive times, it pays to slow down." Rick Stine, managing editor of the Dow Jones News Service, couldn't have agreed more. "This is the first time I'm glad to say that Bloomberg beat me on a story," he said.

Sources: Associated Press, *B.U. Bridge,* Newsbytes, *New York Times,*
Online Journalism Review, Reuters, *USA Today,*
U.S. Securities and Exchange Commission, *Wall Street Journal*

What would you do if you spotted an error on an on-line auction site that would allow you to walk away with a beautiful car for an unrealistically low price? Would you take the car or would your conscience stop you from taking advantage of someone else's misfortune? For an office worker in Shanghai, the decision was an easy one. He took the car.

A WHEEL DEAL

EachNet, China, Summer 2002

This story begins in the summer of 2002, when Han Bin of Shanghai, China, spotted a secondhand Volkswagen Passat while visiting EachNet.com, a popular Chinese auction site. For reasons that are not entirely clear, Han was able to put in a cheap bid of $14 (U.S.) for the car, which was valued at around $12,000 (U.S.).

No one else outbid him, so Han won the auction for a measly $14. He subsequently received a confirmation e-mail from EachNet informing him that he was the successful bidder. But Yongda Automobile Sales, the company that was selling the vehicle, wasn't about to give in without a fight.

The company argued that the auction was an obvious mistake, since there was no way they would have sold a $12,000 car for only $14.

"It's unbelievable. We're trying to find out how this could have happened," said Zhu Baocheng, a Yongda marketing executive who was quoted by Reuters. "We've tried to talk to Han, but he's been very stubborn. Most people in his situation would be stubborn," he added.

Yongda tried to stop the transaction from proceeding, but Han refused to cooperate and took the unusual case to Shanghai district court. According to EachNet, human error was the likely cause of the mishap, since the car had apparently been listed for sale in an area of the Web site where no minimum sale price was required.

Whatever the cause, the Chinese courts are trying to sort through the mess, which is unprecedented in China. Meanwhile, Han is keeping his fingers crossed, hoping that his first tank of gas will cost more than the car itself.

Sources: Agence France-Presse, EachNet.com, Reuters, *Shanghai Star*

It's the kind of catastrophic mistake that makes you recoil in horror when you realize what you've just done. In April 2000, an oil company in Wisconsin accidentally pumped 100 gallons of home heating oil into the wrong person's home. And to make matters worse, the sticky, smelly substance was pumped right onto the floor of the home's newly renovated basement, which had just been turned into a brand-new family room.

A SLICKY SITUATION

Riiser Energy, April 2000

The unlucky homeowners, Gregory and Julie, used to have their home heated by oil, but they had switched heating systems and removed their fuel tank shortly before the basement was remodeled. The couple had canceled their service contract with Riiser Energy, their oil supplier, and the deliveries had stopped.

But eighteen months later, an unexplained computer glitch at Riiser caused a delivery order to be mistakenly generated for the couple's home. The unsuspecting driver showed up and attached the fuel pump to the home's external fill pipe, which had never been removed. Unaware that there was no fuel tank inside the home, the driver turned on the flow of oil and it gushed right into Gregory and Julie's basement, just like lava from a volcano, saturating the carpet, furniture, dry wall, and everything else in sight.

When Julie got home from work that day, she was stunned by what she saw. The basement was covered in pink goop and the unmistakable odor of fuel oil permeated the entire house. Unable to bear the smell, the couple were forced to temporarily move out of their home while the fumigators and contractors moved in to repair the damage. The newly finished basement couldn't be salvaged and had to be completely rebuilt from scratch.

Riiser Energy was deeply apologetic for the computer glitch. "It's every oil company's nightmare," said Dave Frankhart, Riiser Energy's vice president, who was quoted by the Associated Press. He said the cost of fixing the damage "would be taken care of."

For their part, the homeowners no doubt realize their experience could have been much worse. It could have been a demolition company with the computer problems!

Source: Associated Press

> A woman in Taiwan wound up in the emergency room of a local hospital after taking the term "phone sex" much too literally.

GOOD VIBRATIONS

Taipei, Taiwan, February 2001

The woman had been fooling around with her boyfriend when he inserted a Nokia 8850 cell phone up her backside. The couple had apparently been experimenting with the phone's vibrating function, which was triggered each time the boyfriend called her number. They thought the phone would be a cool sex toy, but the plan backfired after the cell phone slipped inside the woman and she started having severe abdominal pains.

The woman was rushed to the Taipei Medical University Hospital, where the cell phone was found lodged in her bottom.

Incredibly, this wasn't the first time that doctors at the hospital had been witness to this type of bizarre medical case. The previous week, another woman had arrived in the emergency room with a phone stuck

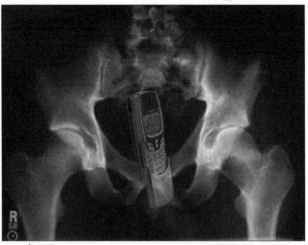

A humorous depiction of what doctors in Taipei might have seen when they took an X-ray of a patient complaining of abdominal pain. The unidentified woman was discovered to have a cell phone lodged in her buttocks.

in her bottom. When questioned by medical staff, the embarrassed patient explained that she had sat on the phone by accident.

In both cases, doctors were puzzled by the choice of a cell phone as a sex toy. "We were all wondering why. Well, we guessed it's because some mobile phones have this vibrating function," said the hospital spokesperson.

When asked to comment on the newfound use for their mobile phones, Nokia refused to give an official statement, but they didn't discourage the practice either. "It's very strange. People can do many things with their mobile phones," a spokesman told the *South China Morning Post*. "We can't control how the users use their phones. It's just a personal issue."

Sources: e-mail correspondence, *Register, South China Morning Post, Taipei Times, Toronto Star*

> nited Airlines may fly the friendly skies, but the airline wasn't so friendly when Eric Bescher caught them selling tickets to Europe for less than the price of a good bottle of wine.

PLANE MISTAKES

United Airlines, January 2001–May 2002

Bescher, a frequent flier with United Airlines, was browsing the United Web site on the evening of January 31, 2001, looking for a cheap ticket to Europe in March. Pricing a round-trip fare from San Jose, California, to Paris, he was stunned to see that the total price was $27.98!

It turned out that a bug had hit United's computers. Instead of quoting the correct ticket prices, United's Web site was showing customers fares that included only taxes and some miscellaneous fees.

The bug also caused fare prices to bounce around like share prices on NASDAQ. To the delight of on-line shoppers, quotes for the exact same ticket changed from minute to minute.

While Bescher was coming to terms with what had just happened, other users of United's Web site were experiencing similar strokes of luck.

It wasn't long before word of the bargain fares spread to chat rooms and message boards on the Internet.

At 7:09 P.M. on January 31, a user named Benjamin shared his discovery on FlyerTalk.com, a popular on-line chat room for travelers.

"I was looking around for trips from SFO [San Francisco] or SJC [San Jose] to Paris. I stumbled across a fare for $85.42 and booked it (twice). Can United pull this back and claim it was a mistake?" he asked.

Benjamin's note sparked a stampede to United's Web site, and a flurry of activity followed on the chat room. Here is an actual transcript of the dialogue on FlyerTalk that evening as other travelers scrambled to take advantage of the incredible fares to Europe. As you read the dialogue, keep in mind that the codes used in the chat room refer to the different airports (SJC = San Jose, CDG = Paris, SFO = San Francisco, LAX = Los Angeles). RT stands for "round-trip."

7:15 P.M.: "If this is true... why don't you grab it... NOW !!!!!!!!!!!!!!!!!!!!!!!!!!!!!!!!"

7:17 P.M.: "I grabbed two of them. Get em' while they're hot!"

7:33 P.M.: "I just checked fare for SJC/CDG for March 3 return March 4th and it priced at 60.96."

7:37 P.M.: "The same flights just priced at 27.98"

7:41 P.M.: "I can't believe I just bought a SJC-CDG RT for $ 27.98"

7:46 P.M.: "I booked two tickets departing 3/9 returning Tue 3/13. SFO-LAX-CDG-SFO"

7:52 P.M.: "I just booked it too for $21.98."

8:00 P.M.: "I got it too...$ 27.59... bought two....headed back for more!"

8:07 P.M.: "Bot 4 more for the following weekend too. $24.98"

8:07 P.M.: "Did not read fast enough. Bought 2 out of SJU for $85 a pop. Should have done SFO for $27"

By 8:10 P.M., the party was over, and United's Web site began quoting regular prices again. But while the accidental seat sale may have ended, the battle had just begun. In the end, 143 people had scooped up the bargain fares during the computer glitch, and many of the travelers had no intention of paying full price for their tickets.

In an interview with the *Wall Street Journal,* United Airlines remained defiant. "Anyone who thought they could fly from L.A. to Paris for $27 should have known better," said Chris Brathwaite, a spokesperson for the airline. "It's clearly a mistake: Everyone knows you don't fly first-class to Paris for $29. You don't get something for nothing."

United's comments deepened the resolve of many of the affected travelers. Eric Bescher, the frequent United flier who got a round-trip ticket from San Jose to Paris for $27.98, was furious when United later billed his credit card for $573. This was in spite of the fact that he had an e-mail confirmation in his possession, confirming the $27.98 fare.

Speaking to the *Wall Street Journal,* Bescher said he planned to fight the charge. "If they don't come through with a goodwill gesture, I'm going to dispute it," he stated. Other recipients of the ridiculously low fares took a similar stance and argued that the fares should be binding, even if they were the result of a computer error.

The *Wall Street Journal* story was picked up by other newspapers across the United States, casting an unwanted national spotlight on United Airlines and the plight of the 143 travelers who were lobbying United to honor their tickets. A small computer bug had suddenly become a public relations nightmare for the airline.

On February 19, United Airlines finally caved in. Rather than enter into a prolonged battle with its customers, United agreed to honor the mispriced tickets. "We believed we were on somewhat solid footing to legally cancel the tickets, but we realized that's an inappropriate way to handle the situation," explained United spokesperson Chris Brathwaite. "We say to them, 'Bon voyage, and enjoy this once-in-a-lifetime opportunity.'"

Unfortunately, to United's chagrin, the company suffered several more high-profile ticket glitches in the months that followed, giving them the dubious distinction of being the most error-prone airline when it came to on-line pricing goofs.

In August of 2001, travelers were able to buy round-trip tickets from Chicago to India for between $120 and $180 as a result of a technical glitch. About 120 lucky travelers snatched up the bargain tickets, which normally sold for as much as $2,500, before United discovered the problem. Then in May 2002, round-trip tickets to U.S. destinations such as Los Angeles and San Francisco mistakenly went on sale for $5 (U.S.). In both cases, United agreed to honor the tickets at the reduced fares.

One California resident was thrilled with United's pricing misfortunes—he got to take his family of three to India for a total cost of $360. "I was planning to pay ten times that," he told the *San Jose Mercury News*. "Now I can do more shopping."

Sources: Associated Press, FlyerTalk.com, *San Francisco Chronicle, San Jose Mercury News, Wall Street Journal*

Although it isn't yet medically possible for a man to become pregnant, several men in England were given a scare in January 2002 that made them think otherwise.

IS IT A BOY OR GIRL?

Chesterfield and North Derbyshire Royal Hospital, January 2002

More than thirty men who were scheduled for operations at Chesterfield and North Derbyshire Royal Hospital in England were contacted by mail and informed that their surgeries had been postponed. The reason? The letters stated that they were pregnant!

Prior to surgery, all patients are required to go through a preassessment examination to identify any health problems that would make an operation unsafe. If the tests reveal any medical reason why the surgery needs to be postponed, the hospital uses a standard form letter to inform patients of the delay.

According to the hospital, the notices were mistakenly generated when a staff member selected the wrong type of letter from a list of predetermined choices stored on the hospital's computer system.

"We realized what had happened as soon as the letters went out," said a spokesperson for the hospital. "It was human error and we have sent a follow-up letter to each patient and their GP. No one has been removed from the waiting list as a result of the letters—they simply received the wrong information. Although some patients have found the letter funny, there is a serious side. The Trust has changed working practices to make sure it can't happen again—to avoid patients receiving incorrect clinical information in the future."

Most of the patients no doubt got a good laugh from the blunder. Cyril Pacey, a seventy-five-year-old grandfather and one of the patients who received the surprising letter, said he was astounded by the news, especially since he wasn't even scheduled to have an operation. "It's certainly a novel way to get the waiting list down," he joked.

Sources: *Mirror,* Reuters, *Yorkshire Post*

This is the story of a woman who was caught with her pants down—literally.

BABY BLUES

America's Health Network, June 1998

On June 16, 1998, a forty-year-old American woman delivered a baby during a real-time Internet broadcast that marked the first time a woman had ever given birth live on the Web. The event sparked worldwide interest, and tens of thousands of people converged on the Web site of America's Health Network, a Florida-based U.S. cable television channel, to watch the birth take place.

The mother, who became somewhat of a celebrity as a result of the broadcast, was not fully identified to the public during the event and was known only by the name Elizabeth. The story was picked up by news organizations across the United States, and Elizabeth's picture was beamed into the homes of millions of people during daily and evening news broadcasts.

As luck would have it, somebody saw her picture and advised police that she was a wanted criminal. Incredibly, there were indeed several warrants for Elizabeth's arrest, on charges of passing bad checks in 1989. When she realized the police were onto her, Elizabeth turned herself in to the authorities.

The media had a field day with this unusual story, which saw a woman go from celebrity status to wanted fugitive in only a few short days. One major news wire ran a story with the headline "Baby Boy Was Not the Only Thing Internet Mom Bounced."

The woman was eventually cleared of the bad-check charges after her lawyer successfully argued that too much time had elapsed since the original charges were filed.

Sources: Agence France-Presse, Associated Press, *Orlando Sentinel*, United Press International

t's not every day that you can gamble on a horse race and be assured of a win. But in mid-2002, a couple of lucky gamblers found themselves in exactly that situation. They had stumbled across a serious glitch on an Australian sports-wagering site that allowed them to place bets on horse races that had already been won.

SADDLED WITH WINNINGS

IASbet Limited Australia, May 2002

The glitch affected the Internet betting site of IASbet, an Australian provider of bookmaking services for racing and sporting events. In May 2002, one of IASbet's customers noticed that its Web site was still accepting bets for races that had already been completed.

Although the customer didn't inform IASbet of the error, he initially didn't take advantage of the situation either. But when he returned to the betting site two weeks later and discovered that the problem hadn't been fixed, his excitement got the best of him, and he bet on a race where the winning horse was already known.

The unidentified gambler exploited the glitch at least one more time and racked up close to $10,000 in winnings before IASbet officials shut him down. He was subsequently ordered to repay all the money or else face legal action.

A number of other sharp-eyed bettors profited from the computer flaw as well, but IASbet said the money involved wasn't substantial.

Source: *Australian*

When a hacker breaks into a Web site, the result is often ugly. Most computer hackers deface the Web sites they break into, destroy data, and/or steal any valuable information they can find, such as passwords or credit card numbers. But sometimes all a hacker wants to do is pull off a great prank.

QUACK A SMILE

Universal Studios, May 1997

One of the most humorous Web site break-ins ever to occur happened on May 27, 1997, when an apparent hacker broke into the Web site of the film *The Lost World: Jurassic Park*. *The Lost World* was the much-anticipated sequel to Steven Spielberg's 1993 smash hit, *Jurassic Park*.

When the vandal broke into the site on May 27, he or she replaced the film's official logo with a picture of a duck and humorously changed the title to *The Duck World: Jurassic Pond*.

In an interview at the time, Alan Sutton, vice president for distribution and marketing at Universal Studios, the company distributing the movie, said he found the hacker's handiwork "amusing." He said he had no plans to go after the culprit because the Web site was altered "in a spirit of fun."

Some people, however, were convinced that the hack attack was an inside job and a ploy by Universal Studios to generate publicity for the movie.

The Web site of The Lost World: Jurassic Park—*before the break-in.*

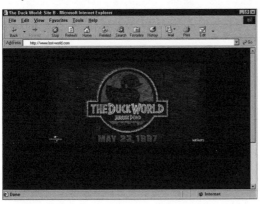

The Web site of The Lost World: Jurassic Park—after *the break-in.*

To this day, the jury is still out on whether the incident was a real crime or just a publicity stunt.

Sources:
CNN, Reuters

Computer prices are dropping all the time, but when Compaq Australia's Web site started selling some high-end laptops for a penny each in May 2002, customers must have thought they were seeing a mirage.

A PENNY FOR YOUR COMPUTER?

Compaq Australia, May 2002

Either Compaq was desperate for business or something had gone terribly wrong with the company's pricing system. Regardless of the explanation, customers weren't about to let these bargain-basement prices pass them buy. Several on-line shoppers scooped up the Compaq laptops for a savings of several thousand dollars apiece.

Matt Cust, an on-line shopper, was one of the first to stumble across the one-cent laptops. He quickly spread news of his discovery in an on-line chat room, and Compaq Australia was quickly flooded with additional orders from bargain-hungry shoppers. "People were ordering ten at a time," said Cust, who was interviewed by ZDNet Australia, an on-line computer publication. "At one cent a go, that's ten cents, so why wouldn't you?"

It turned out that the one-penny laptops were indeed caused by a computer glitch, and Compaq rushed to fix the pricing error as soon as they became aware of the mistake. However, by the time the correct prices were reinstated, several hundred customers had apparently taken advantage of Compaq's misfortune.

According to Cust, more than 500 laptops were purchased for a penny each, although Compaq later disputed that number, saying the number of sales was more like 200. Either way, Compaq was facing a loss of tens of thousands of dollars, and the company wasted no time putting an end to the folly.

Every affected customer was e-mailed by Compaq and told that the company wouldn't be honoring the pricing mistake. "Unfortunately, due to a system error, certain Presario notebooks were posted to our Web store last night (May 2) for a price of $0.01 instead of their usual sell prices of $2,799 or $3,999," the e-mail said.

Compaq obviously hoped the matter would end there, but several greedy customers threatened to slap the company with a class-action lawsuit unless Compaq agreed to honor the prices that had been published on their Web site.

"We've printed out the receipt and looked at the terms and conditions on [Compaq's] Web site which say that all sales are final and binding as soon as you push the 'sale' button," said Matt Cust, the customer interviewed by ZDNet and one of the individuals spearheading the legal battle against Compaq.

In a written statement, the company fought back, arguing that the low prices were obviously too good to be true and no reasonable person could have assumed that Compaq was actually selling their laptops for a penny. But Matt Cust and his followers were adamant that they weren't about to give in.

"We're trying to pressure Compaq into honoring at least some of it—maybe one laptop each person," he said. But Cust and his group later threw in the towel, realizing that their chances of victory were slim.

Sources: *Age,* Matt Cust, ZDNet Australia

> 've searched high and low for the funniest
> technical-support call in the world and I think I've
> found it—in the tiny mountainous nation of Costa Rica.

ONCE UPON A FARM

Del Monte Foods, Costa Rica, January 2002

The call was placed from a farm that is part of the Costa Rican operations of Del Monte, one of the world's largest producers of fresh fruit and vegetables. In January 2002, an employee had a problem with a malfunctioning computer, so he called one of the company's computer technicians and described the "error" message that kept popping up on his screen. The technician listened to the problem and then dispatched a driver to go and pick up the machine.

The technician was baffled when the driver returned with the employee's computer monitor but nothing else. His first thought was the driver had made some sort of mistake or picked up the wrong piece of equipment, so he called the employee for an explanation. "Why did you only send me the monitor?" the puzzled technician asked.

In total seriousness, the employee replied, "The monitor was the only part showing the error."

Sources: *Computerworld,* Del Monte

When Disney released its much-hyped *Toy Story* DVD collector's set in October 2000, the company really fouled up.

IS THIS THE DIRECTOR'S CUT?

The Walt Disney Company, October 2000

Buyers of the boxed DVD set got an unexpected surprise when they watched one of the discs and encountered a scene from the adult-rated film *High Fidelity*. That wouldn't have been such a bad thing if the clip didn't show John Cusack uttering two expletives.

The collector's edition, packaged as "Toy Story: The Ultimate Toy Box," contained three discs, including *Toy Story, Toy Story 2,* and a bonus disc with behind-the-scenes footage and commentary by director John Lasseter.

On the *Toy Story 2* disc, an obscene excerpt from *High Fidelity* appeared suddenly and unexpectedly in the middle of the film. One mother quoted by ABC News said her two young sons were watching

Toy Story 2, when *High Fidelity* suddenly appeared on the screen and foul words began spewing from John Cusack's mouth.

"I heard a couple of swear words that I don't think [my sons] ever heard and am not sure they knew what they were, so I just got them out of the room as fast as I could," the bewildered woman said.

Disney discovered that the dirty clip had been inserted into *Toy Story 2* as a result of a manufacturing glitch at Technicolor Videocassette, the company that produced the DVDs for Disney. Fortunately, the botched DVDs were distributed only to Costco stores in the United States, so the damage was somewhat contained.

Although most of the discs were quickly pulled off the shelves and sent back to Disney, some remain in viewers' homes, no doubt destined to be true collector's editions one day.

Sources: ABC News, Associated Press, E! Online, *Los Angeles Daily News, Tampa Tribune, Variety*

It's rather ironic that a company devoted to chronicling human knowledge would succumb to information overload. But it happened to Encyclopaedia Britannica in 1999, marking one of the most embarrassing moments in the company's 236-year history.

"C" IS FOR "COLLAPSE"

Encyclopaedia Britannica, October 1999

Encyclopaedia Britannica is, of course, one of the best-known reference publishers in the world. Their flagship thirty-two-volume encyclopedia was first published in 1768, and the company's products are found in millions of homes, libraries, and businesses.

In the mid-1990s, Encyclopaedia Britannica's business was in decline and the company was at a crossroads. Not only was the company trying to figure out how to deal with the Internet, which posed a real threat to their survival, but they faced stiff competition from Microsoft, which began giving away their CD-ROM encyclopedia, Encarta, to personal computer buyers.

On October 19, 1999, in an obvious act of desperation, Encyclopaedia Brittanica stunned the business world by announcing that their entire thirty-two-volume encyclopedia was now available on the Internet free of charge. Revenues, the company said, would now come from advertising banners on their Web site.

The reaction from the public was swift—and unimaginable.

Starting on the day of the historic announcement, Encyclopaedia Britannica's Web site was flooded by a "tidal wave" of millions of visitors, causing the site to collapse under the load.

Incredibly, more than *10 million* Web users attempted to access the site, but only 100,000 were able to reach the first page. According to the Lycos search engine, Britannica.com was so popular the week of launch that they received even more search queries than actress Pamela Anderson, the Internet's most searched-for celebrity.

Facing a crisis of incredible proportions, Encyclopaedia Brittanica appealed to its customers and asked them to be patient.

In a letter published on the site, the company apologized for the inavailability of its promised Web site. "In many ways, we have truly been victims of our own success. . . . We had no idea that this volume of traffic would be achieved so quickly."

The site remained clogged for more than a week as Encyclopaedia Britannica's staff as well as outside consultants worked around the clock to add more computer servers and extra capacity. Although Britannica.com was eventually reopened to the public, the company became the laughingstock of the business world for mishandling their high-profile launch, and newspapers had a field day with the story. "So far, Encyclopaedia Britannica Inc.'s much-touted new Web site has been a real bomb.com," wrote the Associated Press. The *Globe and Mail* in Canada couldn't resist adding their own bit of humor to the story. Their story ran with the headline "Britannica Site Found under 'I' for Invisible."

But Encyclopaedia Britannica said they would have looked like fools had they invested the kind of money the site actually needed on launch day. "No one in his right mind would have built an infrastructure capable of

The letter of apology that appeared on Encyclopaedia Britannica's Web site after it crashed in October 1999.

addressing the demand we had in the first day," Jorge Cauz, Encyclopaedia Britannica's chief of marketing, told the *Chicago Tribune*.

He may have been right, but Encyclopaedia Britannica's error in judgment has earned the company its own place in the annals of world history—as one of the most memorable Web site collapses ever.

Sources: Associated Press, *Chicago Tribune*, *Globe and Mail*, *Los Angeles Times*, Reuters

> n 1998, a start-up Silicon Valley company called Centraal Corporation was poised to launch a new software product that promised to revolutionize how Internet users could search for information on the World Wide Web. The product, called the Real Name System, would allow Internet users to type names into their Web browsers rather than long, cumbersome Web addresses. For example, an Internet user seeking information on Volkswagen's Beetle could simply type the word "Beetle" into the address window on his or her browser and go right to Volkswagen's Web site.

OH, DEER!

Centraal Corporation, March 1998

The company planned to make money by encouraging businesses to register specific names or trademarks for forty dollars each. For example, Disney could register the name Mickey Mouse so that anyone entering that name would be immediately connected to Disney's Web site. In order for the service to work, Internet users would need to download software that would match the names registered by participating companies with their Web sites.

After months of tireless development, launch day finally arrived and Centraal Corporation was ready to unveil their breakthrough product at a major trade show in Los Angeles. As reporters crammed into the room that had been set up for the press conference, the excitement was building. This was the moment the company had been working toward for months.

The press conference got under way and Centraal demonstrated how their revolutionary new addressing system would make it easier for Internet users to find information on the World Wide Web. The company used the Disney movie *Bambi* as an example of how their new system could benefit advertisers. Centraal explained that if an Internet user wanted to go to Disney's *Bambi* site, all the person would need to do was to type the word "Bambi" into his or her Web browser. The company explained that their new Internet addresses would be so easy to remember, even a child could use them.

The *Bambi* example subsequently appeared in a Reuters story describing the launch of the Real Name System. It wasn't long before hundreds of excited people, having read about the launch, decided to try out the new service. However, most Internet users didn't realize they needed to download special software first. Using the example contained in the news article, they simply typed the word "Bambi" into their Web browsers. Around the same time, a journalist who had attended the press conference also decided to try out Centraal's new service. Following the example used in the press conference, she, too, typed "Bambi" into her Web browser to see what would happen.

The result was both shocking and embarrassing. Internet users who typed the word "Bambi" into their Web browsers found themselves on a racy porn site with scantily clad women. Needless to say, there was no sign of the cute deer that Disney made famous—just voluptuous women with barely any clothes on.

Word of the blunder quickly became the talk of the trade show. Reuters also received a "torrent" of angry e-mail messages from Internet users who found themselves being enticed by naked women when they typed "Bambi" into their Web browsers.

"I tried just entering Bambi. Oooooops!" wrote one user who was evidently amused by the gaffe. "THIS AIN'T DISNEY BOYS!" said another amused user. Other people, however, found it hard to see the lighter side of the situation. "I was shocked to see a pornographic Web page pop up instead of the Walt Disney Web page for *Bambi* as you stated in your article," one irate user said to Reuters. "Given that you mention in your lead that these new addresses are something even a child can remember, I think the implications are not what you intended. I'd hate to see kids trying this out and being exposed to this filth."

For Centraal Corporation, their all-important product launch was backfiring before their eyes. They reiterated to the media that the product would work only if their software was downloaded first, but it was too late. The press were going to write about the bungled product launch whether Centraal liked it or not. "For Pornography, Type Bambi," screamed a headline on the Wired News Web site. Even the prestigious *Times* of London couldn't resist getting in on the fun. Their story was headlined "A Change of Address That Could Cost You Deer."

Keith Teare, president of Centraal, meanwhile, was embarrassed about the whole mess. "I think I might not use the *Bambi* example anymore," he said.

Sources: News.com, Reuters, TechWeb News, *Times* (London), Wired News

ere's some good news about airline safety. You don't have to worry about the man-eating toilet that apparently preyed on a woman aboard a Scandinavian Airlines (SAS) transatlantic flight.

FLUSHED WITH ANGER

Scandinavian Airlines, 2001

According to the airline, an American woman flying from Scandinavia to the United States found herself in an embarrassing situation after she was sucked into a toilet aboard the SAS Boeing 767 she was traveling in.

The woman had pressed the flush button while seated, triggering the vacuum mechanism that sucks the waste out of the toilet bowl. The sheer strength of the vacuum pulled her into the toilet and sealed her there. She tried unsuccessfully to remove herself from the seat, but she couldn't budge.

"She could not get up by herself and had to sit on the toilet until the flight had landed so that ground technicians could help her get loose,"

Reuters quoted an airline spokesperson as saying. "She was stuck there for quite a long time."

The incident happened in 2001 and the woman subsequently filed a complaint with the airline, according to the Reuters report.

The Reuters story was fed into newsrooms around the world, including those of hundreds of radio and television stations, newspapers, and Web sites. Soon, everyone was talking about the poor woman's comical ordeal. Of course, the man-eating toilet made airline turbulence seem like a walk in the park by comparison.

But several weeks later, the airline retracted the story, saying that the incident had never happened. The airline explained that the scenario may have been offered up as a hypothetical emergency during a training exercise.

"We have now checked through all our complaints and claims and we have not been able to locate such an incident," a SAS spokesperson said. "It's the sort of story that may have been used during training when you think of an extreme example of what the crew should do when such and such a thing happens."

But that may not be the whole truth either. The incident was originally reported in a Norwegian daily newspaper in a story about airline passenger complaints. A press official at SAS told me that the story was fed to the media by SAS's public relations department, which had received the information from an internal source who thought it was true. "SAS believed this story was true but found out after a couple of days that it was a hoax," she said.

While SAS didn't want to comment any further about the source of the hoax or how it happened, they did want to reassure their passengers that their toilets were safe. "The important thing is, passengers should not worry about using the bathroom on SAS flights," the airline said.

Sources: Airline Industry Information, Reuters, Scandinavian Airlines

A German couple out driving on Christmas evening had the shock of their lives when they blindly followed the instructions provided by their car's onboard navigation computer and ended up plunging into a river.

BRIDGE OVER TROUBLED WATERS

Caputh, Germany, December 25, 1998

The couple was driving a BMW equipped with one of those fancy satellite-controlled navigation systems attached to the dashboard, and they were faithfully relying on the car's computer to provide directions. The driver came upon a ferry crossing at the Havel River in Caputh, six miles from Berlin. Surrounded by darkness, and probably unable to see the river, the unsuspecting driver continued on his way, not realizing that the road had ended. He zoomed down a ferry ramp and drove his luxury car right into the frigid waters of the Havel River.

Fortunately, the fifty-seven-year-old man and his companion weren't hurt in the mishap, but traffic on the river came to a standstill for two hours while the car was plucked out of the cold water.

According to police, the navigation system failed to tell the driver that he couldn't travel over the river by land. He was anticipating a bridge—not a dunk in the water.

"You can't always blindly rely on technology," a coast guard officer was quoted as saying.

Sources: Associated Press, *Boston Herald, Observer*

egendary singer-songwriter Burt Bacharach may know the way to San Jose, but British travel agency Travelcare apparently needs some directions.

THE ACCIDENTAL TOURIST

Travelcare, England, May 2002

When seventy-year-old Trudy Rosenfield of England booked a trip to the United States with Travelcare, she was looking forward to a peaceful and uneventful holiday. But unbeknownst to Rosenfield, her travel agent had made an incredible goof. When booking the flight, the agent had accidentally selected SJO, the airport code for San José, *Costa Rica,* rather than SJC, the airport code for San Jose, *California*.

Rosenfield's remarkable journey began in Manchester, England, when she boarded a Continental Airlines flight to Newark, New Jersey. She then connected to another flight in Newark, which she thought would take her to California. Little did she know that the plane was about to leave the United States and head 3,000 miles away to sunny

Costa Rica. She slept most of the flight, completely oblivious to the mistake that had been made.

While Rosenfield was peacefully sleeping on the Costa Rica–bound airliner, her cousin Alan was waiting in California for her plane to arrive from Newark. But when he checked with the airport to see when Rosenfield's plane would be landing, he was alarmed to learn that there weren't any flights coming in from Newark. Alan immediately called Continental Airlines to investigate, and that's when he found out that his unsuspecting relative was on her way to Central America.

Representatives from Continental Airlines were dispatched to meet Rosenfield when she got off the plane. Even when she was greeted by airline employees, Rosenfield still didn't know she was in the wrong country. According to the *Daily Mail,* a representative from Continental Airlines approached her and said, "Ma'am, you think you are in California, but you are actually in Costa Rica." Rosenfield was stunned and apparently replied, "Oh my God."

As if the surprise of being in a strange country weren't enough, Rosenfield suffered from breathing difficulties and had to be taken off the plane in a wheelchair. The airline put her up in a hotel in Costa Rica and she flew to Houston the next day for a connecting flight to California. But Rosenfield's streak of bad luck continued. A storm blew into Houston and her flight was delayed, forcing Rosenfield to stay in a hotel for a second night.

Rosenfield finally made it to California the following day, where she was relieved to be reunited with her cousin. A spokesperson for Travelcare told the *Express* newspaper that the mistake was highly unusual. "This is not a mistake that we make regularly," he said. "It's the first such case that I have ever heard of."

Sources: *Daily Mail, Daily Telegraph, Express*

You can say all you want about Regis Philbin and the ill-fated run of *Who Wants to Be a Millionaire* in the United States, but at least the American version of the popular game show hires technicians who know what they are doing.

RICHES TO RAGS

Who Wants to Be a Millionaire **(Thailand), March 2002**

The same cannot be said for the Thai incarnation of the game show, which mixed up the cable connections on the stage and accidentally fed the contestant the answers intended for the host. The contestant in the hot seat at the time was forty-four-year-old street vendor Lertlak Panchanawaporn.

Each time the host read a question, Panchanawaporn saw the correct answer highlighted in green on her screen. As a result, she was able to correctly answer all sixteen questions and win the grand prize of 1 million baht ($23,100 [U.S.]). The show's producers were impressed with Panchanawaporn, yet were suspicious of her amazing streak of good luck, since she had only a fourth-grade education.

Panchanawaporn was questioned after the show, at which time she confessed that the answers had been showing up on her computer monitor. She said she only became aware of the glitch when she got to the fifth question and noticed the answer she thought was right was highlighted in green.

Although Panchanawaporn was forced to forfeit her win because of the technical goof, she was given the chance to play the game again, this time with the cables plugged in properly. Panchanawaporn said she agreed to give up her jackpot because she didn't want the show to get in trouble. On her second try, Panchanawaporn managed to answer five questions correctly and win 25,000 baht, or about $750 (U.S.).

In yet another twist to this humorous story, Celador International, the company that owns the rights to *Who Wants to Be a Millionaire,* issued a statement to make it clear that the Thai version of the show is an unofficial version of the show and not licensed by Celador. They said this type of glitch couldn't happen on their shows because the technology they use is better.

"The computer systems developed by Celador and used across the world within licensed *Who Wants to Be a Millionaire* productions use sophisticated technology that safeguards against any mistake of this kind," a Celador spokesperson said. And that's their final answer.

Sources: Associated Press, BBC News, Reuters

Producers of the theater production of *The Invisible Man* probably thought they had prepared for every possible contingency, but there was one emergency they never expected in their wildest dreams.

A NOT·SO· INVISIBLE GLITCH

Oldham Coliseum Theatre, Lancashire, England, May 2002

When a technical glitch knocked out the lights at the Oldham Coliseum Theatre in Lancashire, England, in May 2002, the Invisible Man literally became invisible.

The actor portraying the Invisible Man in the H. G. Wells production wore bandages so that the audience could see him. But when the lights failed, he, along with everything else, disappeared completely from view.

Technicians immediately went to work on the problem. But by 6:15 P.M., they were still unable to restore lighting to the theater, and the show had to be canceled. Everyone in the audience was offered a free drink and the show was able to continue the next day without incident.

Sources: Reuters, *Scottish Daily Record*

> The following story, while outrageously funny, is possibly an urban legend. It was originally reported by the U.K. publication *Computer Weekly*, but it hasn't been independently verified by any other major news publications.

"DEAR HAPLESS EMPLOYEE: YOU'RE FIRED!"

England, 1993

It's common practice in the world of computer programming to insert dummy names into computer programs for testing purposes. In 1993, a computer programmer at a bank in England made an innocent mistake that made him the laughingstock of the computer industry, embarrassed his employer, and ultimately cost him his job.

The unidentified bank wanted to send a direct-mail piece to their wealthiest customers and promote some of the bank's services. The programmer was asked to write a computer program that would extract the names of the bank's wealthiest customers from the bank's records and generate a form letter for each customer. To test the program, the programmer created a fictitious customer called "Rich Bastard."

Unfortunately for the programmer, and the bank, the test salutation somehow found its way into the actual mailing and two thousand of the bank's most valuable clients received a letter that began, "Dear Rich Bastard . . ."

The bank apparently didn't have a sense of humor and the programmer was reportedly fired for his mistake.

Source: *New Scientist*

How many topless women appear in the Disney movie *The Rescuers*? Just one, but it was enough for Disney to recall 340,000 VHS copies of the film, the first time in the company's history that such a large video recall was ordered.

AN
EM·BARE·ASSING
RECALL

The Walt Disney Company, January 1999

The recall was ordered in January 1999 after it was revealed that a woman's bare breasts could be seen in the window of a building during a scene in the movie, about thirty-eight minutes into the film. The image can't be seen by the naked eye when the movie is run at normal speed because it appears in only 2 frames of the film. To put that into perspective, the movie contains about 110,000 frames and normally runs at 24 frames per second.

Remarkably, the image has apparently been in the movie ever since *The Rescuers* premiered in theaters in 1977. No one noticed the x-rated image then or when the movie returned to theaters for another run in 1983 and then again in 1989. Disney believes that an employee must have slipped the naughty image into the master copy of the animated film sometime in 1976 or 1977. Although a video of *The Rescuers* was first released in 1992, the naked woman doesn't appear because the movie was cut from a different "print."

It remained undetected until 1999, when an animator noticed the image while playing the movie frame by frame. He posted his finding to an Internet discussion group, sending embarrassed Disney officials into damage control.

Disney offered refunds to customers who purchased the video containing the racy image, but reportedly few people took advantage of the offer. I wonder why?

Sources: *Chicago Sun-Times, Dallas Morning News, Entertainment Weekly, Los Angeles Daily News, Washington Post*

> Consider the following odds: Your chances of being struck by lightning are 280,000 to 1; your odds of being killed by a venomous snake, lizard, or spider in any given year are about 20,000,000 to one; and your chances of hitting two holes in one in a single round of golf are about 9,222,500 to 1.

A "STUCK" JURY

Westchester County Courthouse, New York, May 2001

That brings us to the following question: What do you think the odds are of a jury getting stuck in an elevator while on their way to hear a case involving a malfunctioning elevator? It has only ever happened once. In May 2001, a New York State judge was presiding over a case at the Westchester County Courthouse in White Plains, New York, when the jury became stuck in the building's elevator.

The case at hand involved a company in Queens, New York, that was being sued by a nurse and a nurse's aide. The medical workers were seeking compensation for injuries they allegedly suffered after getting stuck between floors in a hospital elevator.

As the jurors headed to the courtroom to hear the case, they found themselves stuck in the elevator. Although they weren't trapped for long, one juror was so freaked out by the incident that she apparently needed an hour to regain her composure.

Defense attorneys promptly went before the judge and argued that the unusual event might prejudice the jury. The judge agreed and declared a mistrial, and a new panel of jurors was selected.

In an interview with the press, defense attorney Thomas Cerussi said the freak occurrence was "pretty ironic." "We really didn't have to twist [the judge's] arm too much," he said.

Sources: Associated Press, *Columbus Dispatch, Newsday, Providence Journal*

pening a box of Honey Nut Cheerios one day recently to find a computer game inside, I realized just how much the cereal industry has changed during the past few decades. When I was little, it was exciting to dig my hands inside a box of cereal and pull out a colorful plastic toy. Today's kids, on the other hand, think nothing of getting shiny, fully loaded CD-ROMs in their cereal boxes. It makes a lowly plastic toy seem lame by comparison.

YUMMY O'S AND COUPON WOES

General Mills, February 1992

ut as generous as today's cereal premiums have become, they still can't top the surprise that eighty-one-year-old Audrey Henning of Calamus, Iowa, found inside her box of Cheerios one day in February 1992. Henning's great-granddaughter was trying to pour herself some cereal one morning and she couldn't get any cereal to come out of the box.

When Henning came over to investigate, she found the box was filled with dozens of coupons—340 in all—each worth fifty cents off assorted varieties of General Mills cereal. Naturally, Henning was flabbergasted.

Two local newspapers, the *Quad-City Times* in Davenport, Iowa, and the *Observer* in DeWitt, Iowa, wrote stories about Henning's unusual discovery, which General Mills attributed to a bizarre glitch on their assembly line. The Associated Press picked up the story, and Henning immediately began fielding calls from news organizations all over the country.

One of the more memorable interviews was a thirty-minute piece Henning did with a radio station in Arizona. "She just wouldn't stop talking," joked Henning's daughter-in-law. But perhaps the ultimate compliment was paid to Henning by the world-famous television game show *Jeopardy!* When *Jeopardy!* producers heard about Henning's odd find, they turned her experience into a clue on the show.

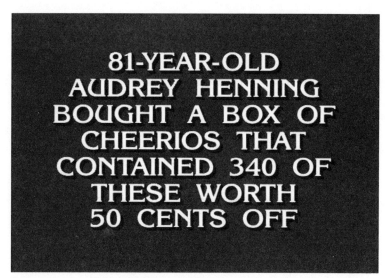

81-YEAR-OLD AUDREY HENNING BOUGHT A BOX OF CHEERIOS THAT CONTAINED 340 OF THESE WORTH 50 CENTS OFF

Audrey Henning of Calamus, Iowa, found 340 coupons in her box of cereal one morning. Her unusual discovery was turned into a clue on Jeopardy!

Despite her coupon bounty, Henning wasn't about to let General Mills off the hook. "There was some cereal in the bottom and a little bit on top, but I told them I got gypped," said Henning, according to the Associated Press. General Mills was quick to make amends, and they sent Henning a Betty Crocker cookbook and some plastic toys for her great-grandchildren. General Mills said it was the first time in their history that such a glitch had happened to a customer.

So what did Henning do with all the coupons? They were hers to keep, and she generously distributed them among friends and relatives. If Henning had kept all the coupons for herself, it would have taken her a whopping twenty-eight years to use them up, assuming she redeemed one coupon a month.

Sources: Associated Press, Audrey Henning's daughter-in-law, Sony Pictures Television

PART 4

TELECOM SNAFUS

When James Storrie of Auckland, New Zealand, opened his monthly mobile phone bill in early 2002, he nearly fell over. It wasn't the amount of the bill that shocked him—it was the message inside.

THE ULTIMATE REVENGE

Telecom New Zealand, February 2002

Printed under the "Rental and Activity" section of Storrie's statement was a $337.50 (N.Z.) charge "for being an arrogant bastard." Storrie was shocked. "How can they speak to their clients like this? It's downright rude," he told the *New Zealand Herald* in an interview.

Storrie couldn't understand what he could have done to deserve such an insult. He couldn't think of any friends at the phone company who might have pulled this stunt as a practical joke, nor did he have any enemies there that he was aware of.

His only recent encounter with the phone company had been the previous week, when he had complained about his mobile phone being

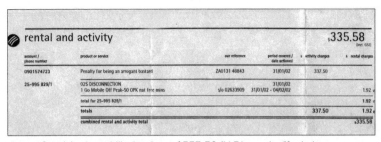

rental and activity   ₁335.58
(inc. GST)

account / phone number	product or service	our reference	period covered / date actioned	activity charges	rental charges
0901574723	Penalty for being an arrogant bastard	ZA0131 48843	31/01/02	337.50	
25-995 829/1	025 DISCONNECTION 1 Go Mobile Off Peak-50 OPK nat free mins	s/o 02633909	31/01/02 31/01/02 - 04/02/02		1.92
	total for 25-995 829/1				1.92
	totals			337.50	1.92
	combined rental and activity total				₁335.58

James Storrie's phone bill, showing a $337.50 (N.Z.) penalty "for being an arrogant bastard."

disconnected. He was told that his service had been cut off because the phone had been reported stolen, but Storrie said he had never made such a report.

Telecom New Zealand officials were horrified at the offensive message but also at a loss to explain how it could have appeared on a customer's bill. "As far as we were concerned, it couldn't happen," a bewildered Telecom spokesperson told the *New Zealand Herald*. The company nevertheless offered Storrie a "confidential compensation package," along with their apologies, and immediately launched an investigation into the unusual incident.

It didn't take long to find the culprit. Within a matter of days, the phone company discovered that a former employee had committed the devilish act on his last day of work. It was unclear whether the employee had a grudge against Storrie or whether he had simply targeted Storrie as part of a random prank.

Because this incident was so unique and undeniably humorous, the story was picked up by the Reuters wire service, which transmitted it to media outlets worldwide. Dozens of radio and television stations and newspapers reported on the "arrogant bastard" story, turning Storrie into an international celebrity.

As for the disgruntled Telecom New Zealand employee, while he may have succeeded in causing Storrie some minor embarrassment, it was Storrie himself who managed to have the last laugh. He found a way to cash in on his newfound fame by selling T-shirts and hats with the phrase, "I complained so I must be an arrogant bastard."

Sources: *New Zealand Herald,* Reuters, James Storrie

Next time you complain about the size of your phone bill, remember Nelson Marotti Filho of São Paulo, Brazil.

WILL THAT BE CASH OR CHARGE?

Telesp, São Paulo, Brazil, April 1999

When Brazil's telecommunications system was privatized in 1998, Spanish telecom giant Telefônica won control of Telesp, the most coveted jewel in the Brazilian telecommunications family. Telesp provides telephone service in the Brazilian city of São Paulo, the largest city in the country.

At the time, Brazilian president Fernando Henrique Cardoso praised the sale, calling the privatization of Brazil's telephone system "one of the greatest privatizations capitalism has ever seen."

Nearly a year later, the news wasn't quite so flattering. Telesp was in the news again, but this time it had committed one of the biggest telephone billing blunders history has ever seen.

In April 1999, Filho got a call from his bank asking how he intended to pay for his monthly phone bill. He said he was stunned when the bank told him he owed a whopping $43 million, just a slight increase from the $31 he really owed.

"I was horrified," Filho was quoted by Reuters as saying. "My bank called me to ask what I wanted to do with the bill. They usually deduct it directly from my account." Of course, Filho didn't have enough money in the bank to cover the hefty charge, so he called his phone company and demanded an explanation for the absurd bill. The company sent him a revised bill and apologized for the mistake, which they said was caused by a technical glitch.

Sources: Agence France-Presse, Reuters

Here's some free advice to couples engaged in passionate lovemaking: Move the telephone off the bed before you do anything. A couple in England learned this lesson the hard way when they accidentally hit their telephone's redial button during a fit of passion in July 1994.

PHONE SEX

Devizes, England, July 1994

The outgoing call was received by a woman in Devizes, England, who picked up the receiver and heard moaning, groaning, and shouting on the line. She figured it was a crank call, so she hung up. But then another call came in, and this time she heard a voice, which she recognized as her daughter's, crying, "Oh my God." A man's voice could also be heard in the background.

The woman immediately tried to call her daughter but kept getting a busy signal. Worried that an intruder was in her daughter's bedroom 100 miles away, the terrified mother called police, and a patrol car raced to the daughter's home to investigate the cries for help. But when authorities arrived on the scene, they found no crime taking place—just a couple making love in the bedroom.

According to police, one of the couple's toes had accidentally pushed the redial button on the telephone while they were making love, prompting the inadvertent call to the woman's mother. It was the mother's number that happened to be in the telephone's memory at the time.

The couple were terribly embarrassed by the incident and both the mother and daughter apologized to the police for the false alarm. The police were relieved that everyone was okay, but they used the incident to warn other lovebirds about the perils of modern technology. "This is a warning for other people," said a police spokesperson. "If you're going to indulge in this sort of thing, move the phone."

Sources: *Independent* (London), Reuters

We've all heard stories about toddlers and pets accidentally calling 911, but the following story is the only one ever recorded where a 911 call came from a tomato.

RIPE FOR TROUBLE

Blacksburg, Virginia, November 1990

One day in November 1990, a 911 dispatcher in Virginia began receiving repeated calls from a home just north of the town of Blacksburg, about 210 miles from the state capital of Richmond. But each time the dispatcher answered the call, there was no one on the line. The mystery deepened when the dispatcher tried to call the home back and got a busy signal. When she hung up, another call came in from the same home, and then another. The puzzled dispatcher grew increasingly alarmed and finally notified the police.

The police tracked down Linda, one of the homeowners, who was visiting her mother at the time. Linda told the police her home should be empty. "I told them I'd locked my house and there shouldn't be anyone in there," she said in an interview with the *Roanoke Times*. The police thought that Linda's home might have been vandalized, so they asked her to come home immediately and meet them there.

When Linda arrived, she was told to wait outside as sheriff's deputies rushed into the home with their guns blazing. They searched the house and found no signs of a break-in. Linda's brother, who had also come to the scene, starting doing some detective work of his own. To everyone's surprise, he discovered that an overripe tomato had been making the frantic calls for help.

The bright and juicy tomato had been sitting in a wire basket above Linda's telephone, leaking juice into her answering machine. Evidently, tomato juice had seeped into the telephone's dialing system and triggered the calls to 911. The police were stumped. "We're not sure how [this happened]," said Chief Deputy Milton Graham of the Montgomery County Sheriff's Office. "Maybe they had speed-dialing and it shorted out," he said.

Linda was also perplexed by the bizarre turn of events. "It was all very strange," she told the *Roanoke Times*. "The police said it was like *The Twilight Zone*. There were several things they did not understand."

For example, they still can't figure out how the answering machine managed to make so many phone calls. "I didn't know the answering machine could even dial out," Linda said. "It's just supposed to take messages."

Sources: Associated Press, *Roanoke Times*

Mementos often come in the most unexpected forms. The grandparents of a British toddler experienced this truism firsthand when their telephone bill turned into an unusual keepsake—a reminder of their grandson Joe's first-ever telephone call.

LITTLE JOE'S FIRST PHONE CALL

London, England, September 1994

In 1994, at the age of one, Joe was playing with his grandparents' telephone, when he accidentally hit the redial button. This caused the phone to make a long-distance call to his relatives who lived 4,000 miles away on the Caribbean island nation of Saint Lucia.

Little Joe never hung up the phone, and the line stayed open for an incredible twenty-five hours, resulting in a total bill of $1,527 (U.S.), or 1,018 pounds.

Joe's grandmother was on holiday in Spain at the time, and Joe and his mother were looking after her house. They had no idea the phone was off the hook until a neighbor alerted them to a possible problem with the phone. From her vacation spot in Spain, Joe's grandmother had been continually trying to call and got worried when she couldn't get through. That's when she called a neighbor to check on the family's welfare.

British Telecom officials explained that the phone should have disconnected after a minute's silence, but sometimes this doesn't happen with overseas calls. They agreed to cancel the charges, much to the relief of the family.

"Joe has always liked the telephone," said Joe's mother in a press interview. "Whenever it rings, he likes to hold the receiver, and the person on the phone has to say hello to him before he's happy. He's got a toy telephone which is his favorite, but we now have to put our own telephone on the window ledge so he can't reach it."

Joe's grandmother, Marion Williams, decided to frame the bill as a souvenir, labeling it "Little Joe's First Phone Call." She said she was "flabbergasted" by the extraordinary phone charge.

Sources: Reuters, *Weekly Journal*

> f you're being robbed and call 911, the California Highway Patrol will be happy to connect you with a police operator—but you may have to listen to some advice on energy conservation first.

DIAL 911 FOR ENERGY·SAVING ADVICE

California Highway Patrol, Summer 2001

elieve it or not, the California Highway Patrol once used the 911 system to recruit new police officers and promote the efficient use of energy.

"You can have an exciting and satisfying career," callers were told. "Make $50,000 a year. Work anywhere in the state. Drive a car, ride a bike, or fly a plane. Your career is waiting for you. Ask for more information when we get back on the line." As if people were going to ask about a career with the police department while their house was burning down!

People who called 911 on their cell phones to report a fire, a medical crisis, or any other type of emergency were subjected to the cheerful messages while waiting on hold for a police operator.

"Oh, sure, I have a gun to my head, and by the way, what about getting a job with the CHP [California Highway Patrol]," a bewildered government official told the *San Francisco Chronicle*. The official was stunned to encounter the message while attempting to report a traffic problem.

Normally, cellular 911 callers would be greeted by a soothing message in English and Spanish telling them to stay on the line for an operator, but the California Highway Patrol told the *San Francisco Chronicle* that a "glitch" had caused the upbeat advertisements to be played continuously instead. The unusual glitch only affected callers in parts of northern California.

Source: *San Francisco Chronicle*

What happens when you place your cellular phone in your fanny pack and go to a football game? As police dispatchers in Fayetteville, Arkansas, will tell you, it's a recipe for trouble, especially if "911" is preprogrammed into one of your one-touch buttons.

BUTTON UP
THAT PHONE!

University of Arkansas, October 1999

On October 9, 1999, the University of Arkansas Razorbacks were playing the Middle Tennessee State Blue Raiders, when the local 911 dispatch center received an avalanche of calls—thirty-five in total—from Razorback Stadium. Each time dispatchers received a call, they could hear cheering in the background, but there was no one on the line. When they tried to call back, no one answered.

Police eventually discovered that the calls were coming from an "excited Arkansas fan" whose enthusiasm for the game had an unintended consequence. The owner of the phone told police that the phone was around his waist and that the calls must have been made accidentally during his repeated standing and sitting motions. Whenever he leaned against his cell phone while cheering, it triggered an emergency call to 911.

Despite the inconvenience caused to police, this story does have a happy ending. The Arkansas Razorbacks won the game 58–6.

Sources: Associated Press, *Boston Herald*

> If you're growing marijuana plants in your home, it's generally not a good idea to call 911.

A DOPEY WAY TO GET ARRESTED

Surrey, British Columbia, Canada, December 2002

But that pearl of wisdom seemed to have escaped a criminal in Surrey, British Columbia, who believed a ridiculous urban legend about wiretapping and foolishly led the police right to her front door.

The unidentified sixty-year-old woman was told by her son that if she dialed 911 followed by the digit 1, she would hear a recorded message telling her if police were tapping her phone. The gullible woman followed her son's advice, but when the 911 operator came on the line, she quickly hung up.

The operator was concerned that something might be wrong at the caller's location, so police were quickly dispatched to the home. When they arrived, they stumbled across a "reasonably sized marijuana-growing operation" inside the house. The woman and three other individuals were immediately taken into custody and later released pending an appearance in court.

A police spokesperson urged the public not to call 911-1 because it would tie up lines needed for people with real emergencies. As the woman in this case discovered, adding the extra digit to "911" still connects you to 911. It does nothing to tell you if your phone lines are being monitored by the police.

It isn't clear if the woman who made the call was on drugs at the time, but it sure seems like it.

Sources: Canadian Press, *Vancouver Sun*

This is a story that Verizon is probably envious of. Or maybe not. Verizon, of course, is the telephone company whose memorable commercials feature an employee traveling the country in a never-ending quest to test the signal quality of the company's cellular phones. From places far and wide, the technician utters the familiar phrase "Can you hear me now?"

JUST PASSING THROUGH

London, England, December 1997

The message Verizon is trying to get across, of course, is that their signal can reach just about anywhere in the United States. It's an advertising campaign that other wireless carriers are envious of. But Orange, a wireless provider in England, has a claim to fame that even Verizon might be jealous of. In fact, it gives new meaning to the term "signal strength."

In December 1997, Rachel Murray of London, England, purchased a cellular telephone to give to her roommate as a Christmas gift. She wrapped the phone and placed it under the tree, but by Christmas morning, it had mysteriously disappeared. The phone was nowhere in sight, but pieces of torn and chewed wrapping paper were scattered all over the floor.

Puzzled, Murray decided to call the number assigned to the cellular phone, hoping the ringing sound would give up the phone's location. She had forgotten the number, so she contacted Orange, the cellular phone's provider, which gave her the number to call.

Murray dialed the number and heard a low-pitched noise, but she couldn't figure out where the sound was coming from. Further investigation led her to her roommate's dog, a five-foot-long bloodhound, who was resting nearby. Murray's first instinct was that the family pet was sitting on the phone. Then, in a moment of incredulity, she realized the ringing sound was coming from *inside* the dog! Murray was stunned.

"I couldn't believe he'd swallowed it. I just sat there in disbelief," said Murray in an interview with London's *Daily Telegraph*.

A local veterinarian told Murray and her roommate that the dog was in no danger and assured them that the telephone would reappear once nature had run its course.

One day later, the dog expelled the telephone as expected. Incredibly, the phone still worked! "We spent most of that night watching him every time he went to the loo. Suddenly it just popped out—we couldn't stay cross for long," Murray said.

A spokesperson for Orange told the *Daily Telegraph*: "It's strange but true. It's amazing where you can get a signal on our phones."

Sources: *Australian, Daily Telegraph,* e-mail correspondence

n January 1992, the Canadian Press told the story of a man in Edmonton, Alberta, whose telephone was affected by a bizarre glitch. His phone kept ringing, but every time he picked up the receiver, there was no one on the line. The ringing continued both day and night, sending the poor man into a frenzy.

FIVE TIMES UNLUCKY

Edmonton, Alberta, Canada, January 1992

e contacted the security department of his local phone company, and they launched an investigation. Naturally, the resident probably assumed that a deranged caller was behind the annoying phone calls.

Not in his wildest dreams did the man expect that the culprit would turn out to be an elevator. The investigation revealed that the calls were coming from an elevator in a hotel, where a malfunction was causing the elevator's security telephone to automatically dial the man's home number each time it went by the fifth floor.

"This was going on intermittently, day and night. The elevator was in a hotel, so you can imagine how many times that would go off when it passes the fifth floor," said Phil Brooks, a telephone company manager, in an interview with the Canadian Press.

Source: Canadian Press

It was a happy moment for a Ukrainian businessman. It was the beginning of 1999 and he had just purchased a pager for each member of his staff as a New Year's gift. He came out of the pager shop, placed the fifty pagers in the backseat of his car, and began driving back to work. Less than 100 meters from his office, all fifty of the devices suddenly went off simultaneously.

RINGING IN THE NEW YEAR

Kiev, Ukraine, January 1999

The shrill sound of the pagers scared him so much that his hands came off the steering wheel and his vehicle careened into a lamppost. After recovering from the crash and inspecting the damage to his car, the bewildered driver looked at the message displayed on each of the pagers. It read, "Congratulations on a successful purchase!"

Sources: Reuters, *Washington Post*

osa Dickson is probably the only person in the United States to have ever run a major city's 911 system from her home.

"GOOD MORNING! I NEED AN AMBULANCE!"

City of Richmond, Virginia, September 1995

t about 5 A.M. on September 26, 1995, Dickson was jolted out of her sleep by the ring of her telephone. She picked up the phone and was surprised to hear a woman on the other end requesting an ambulance. Dickson assumed the caller was probably trying to reach a relative and had accidentally dialed her number by mistake. "Ma'am—you have the wrong number," she politely told the woman.

Dickson hung up, but seconds later the phone rang a second time. It was the same woman asking for an ambulance again. Realizing that the caller was in serious need of help, Dickson asked for the woman's name and telephone number so she could relay the information to emergency personnel. She then hung up and dialed 911. Much to her surprise, the line was busy. It was then that Dickson realized that the city's 911 calls were somehow being directed to her home by mistake.

She immediately called the operator and asked for the nonemergency police number. After being referred to directory assistance, Dickson eventually reached the police and quickly informed them of the problem with the 911 system. "I told them there was a mix-up in the calls," she said in an interview with the *Richmond Times-Dispatch.*

During the next thirty minutes, Dickson calmly sat in her home and fielded emergency calls to 911. Each time, she took the caller's number and passed the information on to the police department.

One female caller gave Dickson a wrong number and when the police couldn't get in touch with her, they called Dickson back. Around the same time, the woman called 911 again, and Dickson was able to get the correct number and pass it on to the police.

As Dickson continued to intercept the city's 911 calls, the police began making preparations to set up an emergency command center in Dickson's home. But much to everyone's relief, the problem was quickly fixed, and Dickson was spared the additional excitement.

A week after being unceremoniously pressed into duty as the city's 911 operator, Dickson was presented with a Richmond City Council proclamation that formally recognized her service to the city. Dickson also received a standing ovation at city hall. "I was just doing my duty," she told the *Times-Dispatch.*

Bell Atlantic said that a software glitch had occurred during maintenance of the phone system, causing 911 calls to be mistakenly diverted to Dickson's residence.

"We've done this one hundred times and never had a problem," a Bell Atlantic account manager told the Richmond City Council. "It's not going to happen again."

Sources: Rosa Dickson, *Richmond Times-Dispatch, Washington Post*

ver since the telephone was invented, we've been incredibly spoiled. At the touch of a button, we can access an operator to help us make collect or long-distance calls. There's no long number to remember and no need to remember how to spell the word "operator." We just dial "0" and an operator comes on the line. That luxury backfired on AT&T in the early 1990s, and the ensuing incident remains one of the most famous toll-free telephone number debacles of all time.

THE NUMBER
THAT SPELLED
TROUBLE

AT&T Corporation, May 1993

n May 1993, MCI introduced 1-800-COLLECT, a new easy-to-remember toll-free number that Americans could use to access MCI's telephone network for the purpose of making collect calls. The rollout was accompanied by a major advertising campaign offering a discount on AT&T's collect-call rates.

A few months later, AT&T introduced their own vanity number—1-800-OPERATOR—and announced their intention to compete directly with MCI's new 1-800-COLLECT service. AT&T also announced that they would immediately begin matching MCI's discounts. The collect-call war between MCI and AT&T had officially begun!

But AT&T never expected what happened next. It turned out that many of us were poor spellers. A lot of people thought the word "operator" was actually spelled "operater." And can you really blame them? When was the last time you had to spell the word "operator" to reach one?

So when AT&T's customers needed to make a collect call, many of them dialed 1-800-OPERATER. That wouldn't have been so bad if the wrong number redirected them back to AT&T. But ironically, that number was owned by MCI. In just the first month of AT&T's program, MCI reportedly raked in more than $500,000 worth of collect call business that was intended for their rival. The debacle became a major embarrassment for AT&T, and many publications couldn't resist poking fun at this classic marketing blunder. One high-tech publication posed the humorous question, "Which Carrier Is Dan Quayle Really Using?"

To add insult to injury, AT&T's research also discovered that 50 percent of those people calling the 1-800-COLLECT number thought it was run by AT&T, not MCI.

Recognizing that their head-to-head battle with MCI had been an unmitigated disaster, AT&T began to publicize a new toll-free number—1-800-CALL-ATT—and advised their customers to stop using the old number.

There was no comment from AT&T when they were asked whether they would sponsor a national spelling bee.

Sources: *BusinessWeek*, MCI, *Network World*, Telecommunications Alert, *Wall Street Journal*

A woman named Nancy from Le Roy, New York, has something in common with teenage actor Haley Joel Osment. Just like Osment's character in the blockbuster movie *The Sixth Sense*, Nancy sees dead people. But she sees her visitors from the dead in a rather unlikely place—on her telephone's caller-ID box.

DEAD RINGER

Frontier Telephone, New York State, February 2002

Scrolling through her telephone's caller display unit one day, she noticed that Thomas Jefferson, Edgar Allan Poe, George Washington, Alexander Graham Bell, and Albert Einstein had called. Naturally, Nancy was freaked out. All the numbers had a 555 prefix with call dates ranging from January 1999 to January 2002. The area codes the calls had supposedly originated from were real—ranging from 202 (Washington, D.C.) to 916 (Sacramento, California).

When Nancy's local telephone provider, Frontier Telephone, heard about their customer's bizarre experience, they insisted there was a logical, not a supernatural, explanation to the phenomenon. A telephone spokesperson explained that dummy names and numbers are routinely preprogrammed into many caller-ID boxes for testing purposes. The dummy information is used to make sure the display works and to ensure the caller-ID unit is functioning properly before it leaves the factory.

According to the spokesperson, any number of events could have caused Nancy's display unit to suddenly list the names of dead presidents and other famous individuals. A malfunction in the caller-ID box, a power failure, and a power surge were just some of the possibilities.

There was no word on whether Nancy had tried to return the calls.

Sources: Associated Press, Frontier Telephone, *Potavia Daily News*

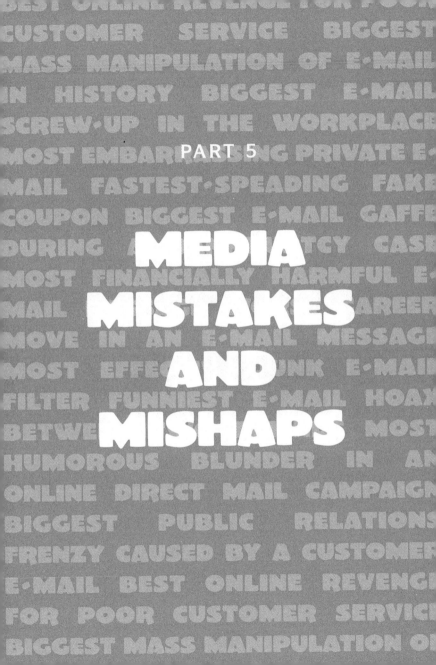

PART 5

MEDIA
MISTAKES
AND
MISHAPS

he competition in the news business is so intense these days, journalists often trip over themselves in their rush to be the first to air with a major news story. Just look at the debacle in Florida during the 2000 U.S. presidential election. CNN initially declared that Al Gore had won the state of Florida. A few hours later, they took back their projection. Later in the evening, they handed the White House to George W. Bush, only to later back off that projection, too. Other television news networks made similar gaffes. "If you're disgusted with us, frankly, I don't blame you," CBS's Dan Rather told his viewers at one point during election night.

RUSH TO JUDGMENT

Time Warner, October 1995

t wasn't the first time in history that the U.S. media embarrassed themselves by prematurely calling an election. For many, the 2000 election mess brought back vivid memories of the 1948 presidential campaign, when Harry S. Truman, the Democratic incumbent, was running against New York governor Thomas E. Dewey, a popular Republican.

Few people thought that Truman had any chance of winning the election that day. In fact, virtually every public opinion poll indicated that Dewey would win, with a margin of victory ranging anywhere from five to fifteen percentage points.

However, much to everyone's surprise, Truman won the election in one of the biggest political upsets in U.S. history. One of the most famous photographs from the campaign is of a jubilant Truman holding a copy of the *Chicago Daily Tribune* from November 3, 1948. The headline reads "Dewey Defeats Truman."

President-elect Harry S. Truman in 1948, holding a copy of the Chicago Daily Tribune *that had prematurely declared his opponent the winner.*

It turned out that the newspaper had made a major gaffe that would become a part of American political history.

How could such a blunder occur? Election returns had come in slowly on the evening of November 2. Despite having incomplete results, staff at the *Chicago Daily Tribune* expected that Dewey would win based on encouraging early poll returns. So the newspaper elected to go to print with a headline proclaiming that Dewey had won the election.

Much to the horror of the *Chicago Daily Tribune,* it later became apparent that Dewey was going to lose—not win—the election. By this time, however, the newspaper had already been delivered to subscribers' homes and newspaper stands.

Staff were quickly dispatched to scour the city and get the newspapers back. Although thousands of newspapers were recovered this way, many copies of the paper went unretrieved and became valuable collector's items.

Almost fifty years later, an on-line media outlet fumbled in a major blunder that has been compared to the classic Dewey-Truman debacle. In October 1995, the world was waiting for the outcome of jury deliberations in the famous O. J. Simpson murder trial. On October 2, the jury reached the verdict after only four hours of deliberations and the judge said that their decision would be announced the following day.

On the morning of October 3, television and radio stations across the United States suspended regular programming and prepared to cover the announcement live. This was also a momentous moment for the Internet. It was the first big news story for the fledgling on-line media industry, and Web sites were anxious to prove that they could handle the challenge of covering a major news event.

As a nervous court clerk read the startling "not guilty" verdict, the Web sites of major news organizations scrambled to be the first to convey the decision to their visitors. However, had you been at Time Warner's Pathfinder Web site, one of the most popular Web sites at the time, you might have seen a different verdict.

To ensure that they could publish the verdict as quickly as possible, Pathfinder had reportedly prepared two graphics—one proclaiming O. J. "guilty" and the other declaring him "not guilty." The apparent plan was to make the correct graphic available as soon as the verdict was known.

Unfortunately, either as a result of poor planning or human error, Pathfinder reportedly made the wrong verdict available to the public— one that showed O. J. Simpson had been convicted of murder. It's not clear whether the "guilty" verdict was mistakenly splashed on the main Web site or whether a clever Web surfer simply found the location where Pathfinder had stored the alternate image. Regardless, it was a major oops for Time Warner.

The wrong verdict made available by Pathfinder.

CNN's Web site, which was sharing the prepackaged graphics with Time Warner, also ran the same incorrect graphic, but in CNN's case, the guilty graphic accidentally went up *before* the verdict was even read. CNN says the error was spotted quickly and the graphic was taken down within thirty seconds. "If anything, we were stunned by being too prepared," said CNN Interactive's editor in chief Scott Woelfel in an interview with *Newsday*.

Embarrassed employees at Pathfinder quickly realized their mistake and yanked the "guilty" image from the site, leaving the "not guilty" graphic instead.

The correct verdict that replaced the original "guilty" image.

But it was too late. Before long, the Pathfinder image containing the wrong verdict was circulating on the Internet, much to everyone's amusement.

"Everyone was mortified," said one Pathfinder employee in an interview with *Newsday*.

It was on-line journalism's first major mea culpa, but it was by no means the last.

Sources: Associated Press, Historybuff.com, *Houston Chronicle*, *Newsday*, telephone interview, *Times* (London), *Wall Street Journal*

ou would think media organizations would have learned their lesson after Time Warner's much-publicized goof with the O. J. Simpson verdict in 1995. But less than two years later, another amusing technical gaffe occurred during a closely watched jury trial. This time, it was ABC News that was at fault.

AN IMPOSSIBLE VERDICT

ABC News, June 1997

On June 2, 1997, all eyes were on a courtroom in Denver, Colorado, as a jury prepared to announce their verdict in the trial of Oklahoma City bombing suspect Timothy McVeigh.

About an hour before the decision was to be formally announced, ABC's Web site news ticker began reporting that McVeigh had been found guilty. Visitors to the Web site were no doubt impressed that ABC had managed to get the verdict so quickly, but other journalists were stunned. How in the world did the television network get such a phenomenal scoop before the verdict had been formally announced?

Visitors who watched the news ticker for a few more seconds saw something even more puzzling. Seconds after reporting that McVeigh had been found guilty, a headline flashed across the screen reporting that McVeigh had been found not guilty. So which was it—guilty or not guilty?

It turned out that ABC had scooped the competition, all right, but it was a scoop of embarrassing proportions. ABC had scooped all of the other networks by becoming the first major news organization to report that McVeigh was both guilty *and* not guilty. Of course, this was impossible, and ABC attributed the whole mess to a technical foul-up on their end.

According to ABC, in anticipation of the verdict being read, they had prepared two alternate headlines for the news ticker—a "guilty" headline and a "not guilty" headline. Both headlines were placed on a "staging" computer, and ABC thought they would be stored there until the actual verdict was known. However, the headlines went live immediately and ABC was caught with their pants down.

An ABC spokesperson explained that their news organization was caught off guard because they had never tried to update the ticker in that manner before. "We've never done the ticker updating this way," she said. "It was not up for very long. Someone noticed immediately and . . . deleted it from the ticker."

Sources: National Public Radio, Salon.com, Wired News

> f you've ever accidentally sent someone an e-mail that you hadn't finished writing, you know how embarrassing that can be.

CRAP ATTACK

Wired News, 1998

Now imagine that you're a journalist, and an unfinished story you're working on inadvertently gets published on the Web. The results can be quite hilarious, as the following story demonstrates.

Sean was a telecommunications reporter at Wired News in 1998 when he was assigned to write a story about a new cable venture by Microsoft cofounder Paul Allen. Allen had just acquired a couple of cable companies, and he was planning to give his new customers access to an array of interactive services ranging from high-speed Internet access to video on demand.

Sean, scrambling to meet a midday deadline, began piecing together the story on his computer screen.

What Sean didn't realize was that the Wired News Web site was about to do an automatic update. While he was in the middle of polishing up his story, the system took the incomplete article off his computer and plastered it live on Wired's heavily trafficked Web site.

Unfortunately, the article that got posted on the Web contained an incomplete paragraph, which Sean recalls read something like, "Allen is betting that cable will be the best pipe into the home for crap."

In a posting to on-line journalism site Poynter.org, Sean explained that the word "crap" was a placeholder that he had inserted into the article draft, reminding him to fill in the sentence later with examples of some of the interactive services that Paul Allen was developing.

The inadvertent publication of the article went unnoticed until Sean heard a panicked cry of "Oh my God!" from a colleague in the office. An editor just happened to be looking at the Web site when he noticed the embarrassing blunder. But it was too late—visitors to the Wired News Web site were already reading the story. Around the same time, Sean got a blistering e-mail from an angry user who couldn't believe what he was reading. "Pipe in the home for crap? What kind of journalism is this?" screamed the e-mail.

As word of the incident spread around the office, Sean was showered with cries of disbelief such as, "Why did you drop an unfinished story into the tool?" and "What the hell were you thinking?"

Sean, who was apparently mortified by the experience, wrote that he eventually completed the story, "once I stopped feeling like I was going to puke."

Source: Poynter.org

On-line newspapers, like their print counterparts, are full of inadvertent typos, grammatical goofs, and wacky headlines. But it's rare that you stumble across an *on-line* typo that makes you howl hysterically. On April 27, 2000, one such error surfaced on the Internet. If there were a Hall of Fame for typographical errors found on the Internet, this notorious gaffe would certainly be an honorary inductee.

SH*T DISTURBER

Reuters, April 2000

Here's what happened. A reporter or an editor at Reuters, one of the world's largest news services, apparently made an embarrassing typographical error that quickly found its way onto some of the most popular Web sites in the world. America Online, Yahoo!, and Excite were among the organizations that published a sports story on April 27, 2000, with the headline "N.Y. Yankees Shit Out Minnesota Twins, 2–0." Of course, the reporter meant to say, "shut out" not "shit out." If you look at a typical computer keyboard, the letter "u" is right beside the letter "i," so it's easy to see how this mistake was made. What a difference a letter can make!

eXcite NEWS
news.excite.com

Excite Home | News Home

Click Here!

Buy Books Now @ Amazon.com!

| News Home | Top News | World | Business | Sports | Entertainment | Tech | Odd | More |

AP • **Reuters** • U-Wire • Canada • Photos • My Sports News

N.Y. Yankees Shit Out Minnesota Twins, 2-0

Reuters Sports News

Updated 9:39 PM ET April 26, 2000

BRONX (Reuters) - Andy Pettitte returned from the disabled list to toss five scoreless innings Wednesday as the New York Yankees defeated the Minnesota Twins, 2-0, for their first shutout of the season.

The Yankees salvaged the final game of their series with the Twins and avoided their first home sweep in a three-game set by Minnesota since 1968.

"I felt good," Pettitte said. "My big concern was trying not to walk batters. I had good command considering the layoff. It felt good to be out there and have my stuff working. I was a little nervous. I was able to block it out once I got out there."

Derek Jeter and Tino Martinez both hit solo homers in the sixth inning to help Jeff Nelson (4-0) get the win for New York, which has won just twice in its last six games and has averaged only 3.5 runs per contest during that span.

"We are happy (Pettitte) is healthy. He pitched well," Jeter said. "It's a plus for the team. We haven't been swinging the bats well. We haven't been playing great. But we have won some games. Hitting is contagious, like pitching and defense."

Nelson moved into a tie with teammate Orlando Hernandez and Boston's Pedro Martinez for the American League lead in wins.

Sosa's Homer Lifts Cubs Over Diamondbacks

Indiana's Smits Suspended for Game 3 of Series

Yankee Great Ford Acknowledges He Has Cancer

Nolan Ryan Leaves Hospital After Bypass

Hobbled Sixers Take on Hornets Again

Reds Release One of the 'Nasty Boys'

Cuba Pitcher Wood to Start Tuesday or Wednesday

Defending NHL Champs Open Series Against Sharks

Dispute Between Bengals, Pickens

A typographical error that had people howling with laughter. Look at the headline.

Once an error gets into a print newspaper, you can't erase it. On the other hand, Internet sites have the luxury of being able to erase mistakes and make them vanish before too many people see them. Fortunately, a few quick-thinking Internet users preserved this classic typo before it was lost to history, forever.

Sources: various Web sites

You may not be aware of the fact that most newswire services (Reuters, the Associated Press, etc.) prepare obituaries for celebrities well in advance of their deaths so that they can quickly move copy over the wire when a celebrity dies. In the news business, it's called a "preparedness." This standard journalistic practice is what led to one of the most talked-about premature death announcements ever to hit the United States.

A NEAR·DEATH EXPERIENCE

Associated Press, June 1998

On Friday, June 5, 1998, a reporter at the Associated Press was updating an obituary for Bob Hope, when a "technical error" caused the death announcement to get accidentally published on the AP's public Web site. The announcement had the word "dead" only in the headline, and blanks appeared where the location of Hope's death and his age would normally have been inserted. This is how the beginning of the story looked to users of the AP Web site that day:

Bob Hope, Tireless Master of the One-Liner, Dead at XX

LOS ANGELES (AP) - Bob Hope, the master of the one-liner and tireless morale- booster for servicemen from World War II to the gulf war, xxxxxxxxxxxxxxxxxxxxx He was xx. (born May 29, 1903).

As soon as the story was published by the Associated Press, a series of comical events began to unfold.

A staff member in House Majority Leader Dick Armey's office saw the AP report and gave it to Armey, apparently oblivious to the mysterious X's that appeared at the top of the announcement.

Armey in turn passed the report on to Representative Bob Stump of Arizona and asked him to announce Hope's death on the House floor. Stump proceeded to make the announcement, which was broadcast live on C-SPAN, a U.S. television network that carries live proceedings from the U.S. House of Representatives and the U.S. Senate. "Mr. Speaker, I have the sad responsibility to tell you this afternoon that Bob Hope passed away," said Stump in his speech to the House.

Journalists across the United States scrambled to cover the story as soon as they heard Stump's announcement. Reuters, a major newswire service, immediately put out a "code red" news flash that Bob Hope had died. The Reuters story was beamed into newsrooms around the world, causing the comedy of errors to continue. Numerous radio shows interrupted their regular programming with the news of Hope's passing. Among the radio networks that jumped on the story was ABC Radio, which issued a national news bulletin shortly after they heard the news from Reuters.

While all of this was going on, the ninety-five-year-old comedian was enjoying breakfast at his home in California, unaware of all the commotion unfolding around him.

The AP's embarrassing goof was eventually noticed by an AP staff member, and the obituary was immediately yanked off the Web site. By then, however, it was too late. Millions of people across the country were already mourning the death of the legendary entertainer.

Word of the mistake eventually got back to Armey and Stump, both of whom apologized to Bob Hope's family for the mistake. Bob Thomas, the AP's veteran Hollywood correspondent, also apologized for the mishap on behalf of his employer.

Hope's daughter, Linda, said they took the whole saga in stride. "[Bob] had a good laugh about it," she told the Associated Press. She said her father had been planning to practice his golf swing in their yard but changed his mind when the media descended on his home. "There are all these news choppers flying around," he said.

Sources: *Arizona Daily Star,* Associated Press, *Los Angeles Times, San Francisco Examiner*

Any journalist worth his or her salt knows the importance of checking sources and fact-checking stories, especially if they come off the Internet. So it came as a surprise when ABC's Peter Jennings used a joke from the Internet and broadcast it as a real news item on ABC's flagship evening news program, *World News Tonight*.

"WE GOT YOU, BABE!"

ABC News, January 1999

At the end of his nightly news broadcast on January 5, 1999, Jennings reported on the funny names given to American movies when they are translated into Chinese. He ended with what he thought was the Chinese title for the movie *Babe*.

"And finally, the new title for Babe reminds us that in China the Communists are still in charge," Jennings told his viewers. "*Babe* is now *The Happy Dumpling-to-Be Who Talks and Solves Agricultural Problems.*"

Unbeknownst to Jennings and his news crew, this translation was complete rubbish and ABC ended up with egg on their face.

This translation had originally come from a farcical article called "The Top 15 Chinese Translations of English Movie Titles." The piece was written in August 1997 by New York resident James Scherer and was contributed to a popular Internet humor site called the Top Five List. In 1997, thousands of people received material from the Top Five List by e-mail, making it one of the more popular e-mail lists on the Internet.

Here is Scherer's list as it originally ran on August 25, 1997:

The Top 15 Chinese Translations of English Movie Titles

15. "Pretty Woman" – "I Will Marry a Prostitute to Save Money"

14. "Face/Off" – "Who Is Face Belonging To? I Kill You Again, Harder!"

13. "Leaving Las Vegas" – "I'm Drunk And You're a Prostitute"

12. "Interview With The Vampire" — "So, You Are a Lawyer?"

11. "The Piano" – "Ungrateful Adulteress! I Chop Off Your Finger!"

10. "My Best Friend's Wedding" – "Help! My Pretend Boyfriend Is Gay!"

9. "George of the Jungle" – "Big Dumb Monkey-Man Keeps Whacking Tree With Genitals"

8. "Scent of a Woman" – "Great Buddha! I Can Smell You From Afar! Take a Bath, Will You?!"

7. "Love, Valour, Compassion!" – "I Am That Guy From Seinfeld So It's Acceptable for Straight People to Enjoy This Gay Movie"

6. "Babe" – "The Happy Dumpling-to-be Who Talks And Solves Agricultural Problems"

5. "Twister" – "Run! Ruuunnnn! Cloudzillaaaaa!"

4. "Field of Dreams" – "Imaginary Dead Baseball Players Live in My Cornfield"

3. "Barb Wire" – "Delicate Orbs of Womanhood Bigger Than Your Head Can Hurt You"

2. "Batman & Robin" – "Come to My Cave and Wear This Rubber Codpiece, Cute Boy"

1. "The Crying Game" – "Oh No! My Girlfriend Has a Penis!"

Reprinted with permission of the Top Five List—chris@topfive.com— http://www.topfive.com.

As a joke, someone took the original e-mail containing the list of fictional Chinese movie titles, deleted all references to the list's origin and inserted it into the text of a real *Wall Street Journal* article about strange translations of English movie titles.

The tampered *Wall Street Journal* article found its way back into cyberspace, where it began to circulate by e-mail. Of course, with the *Wall Street Journal* name attached, people took the Chinese movie titles as fact, not fiction.

ABC News wasn't the only news organization to overzealously report the Chinese movie translations as fact. A handful of other prominent news organizations as well as a Hollywood game show also got taken by the prank.

The *New York Times* was the first victim. James Sterngold, a reporter at the *Times,* received an e-mail from Scott Neeson, a movie executive at Twentieth Century Fox who had read the altered *Wall Street*

Journal article and found it amusing. Neeson thought the entire article was legitimate, so he forwarded it to the *New York Times*.

The *New York Times* reporter, although initially skeptical about the contents of the e-mail, subsequently used several of the ludicrous translations in an article called "Lost, and Gained, in the Translation" that ran on November 15, 1998.

If only the story had ended there. The *New York Times* piece gave the satirical translations instant credibility. After their airing on ABC, they subsequently showed up on CNN, in the *Los Angeles Times,* and incredibly, on *Jeopardy!,* in the form of a clue.

Sterngold said the gaffe was his fault, not Neeson's, and he took the blame for not investigating the story further before publishing it. In an interview with the *Washington Post,* Sterngold said he was embarrassed by his lapse in judgment. "I'm disappointed and depressed," he told the *Post*'s Howard Kurtz. "If it was hard news, I probably would have been more vigilant. But it was a light item."

Kurtz's article ran in the *Washington Post* on December 4, 1998, and appeared on the front page of the paper's Style section. Two days later, the *New York Times* conceded their mistake.

"A brief article on Nov. 15 about the strange things that happen to American movie titles in translation included nine examples erroneously," the correction read. "The nine—translations for 'Leaving Las Vegas,' 'Field of Dreams,' 'The Crying Game,' 'Interview with the Vampire,' 'Babe,' 'My Best Friend's Wedding,' 'George of the Jungle,' 'Batman and Robin' and 'Barb Wire'—were not real releases but spoofs; they appeared on an Internet mailing list and Web site (www.topfive.com) devoted to comedy and edited by Chris White."

For their part, ABC News was also forced to issue an on-air correction for mistaking the titles as real in their January 5, 1999, news broadcast. On January 18, 1999, Peter Jennings retracted the

translation that was originally broadcast but stopped short of apologizing for the blunder:

"And a correction is in order," said Jennings at the end of his broadcast. "Recently, we reported how some American movie titles were translated for audiences in China. We got one of them wrong. The title for the film *Babe* was not actually *The Happy Dumpling-to-Be Who Talks and Solves Agricultural Problems.* For that, it turns out, credit goes to a Web site, TopFive.com. The real title for Chinese moviegoers was *I May Be a Pig, but I'm Not Stupid.*"

All of this just goes to show you how anything posted on the Internet can quickly take on a life of its own. Just remember: If it sounds too bad to be true, it probably is.

Sources: *American Journalism Review, Kansas City Star, New York Times,* TopFive.com, *Washington Post*

hey say money doesn't grow on trees, but tombstones are another matter entirely.

A GRAVE ERROR

San Francisco Chronicle, August 2002

On August 14, 2002, the Web site of the *San Francisco Chronicle* ran an outrageous story about a deceased cattle rancher in Bozeman, Montana, who had a cash-dispensing machine installed in his tombstone so that his relatives would visit him there more frequently.

According to the story, which was originally picked up by a news service called Wireless Flash and subsequently posted on the *San Francisco Chronicle*'s Web site, a man named Grover Chestnut had willed debit cards to some of his relatives and told them they were allowed to withdraw a maximum of $300 per week from the ATM at his grave site.

The article featured an interview with Joel Jenkins, who claimed to work for the company that built the ATM for Chestnut. He said that Chestnut's dreams were already beginning to come true. According to Jenkins, one of Chestnut's granddaughters gave up her pursuit of acting in New York in order to take advantage of the innovative financial security blanket offered by her late grandfather.

A press release issued by Jenkins's company, Living Legacy, suggested that Chestnut's plan was well thought out. To ensure that his relatives visited the grave site personally to receive their weekly inheritance, Chestnut apparently rigged the ATM with a "fingerprint scanning device" to prevent cash from being dispensed to anyone but his legitimate heirs.

The *San Francisco Chronicle* yanked the amusing article from their Web site when they learned that the *Bozeman Daily Chronicle* had done their own investigation and couldn't confirm that anyone by the name of Grover Chestnut had died nearby. Nor could they confirm the existence of Chestnut's granddaughter, the aspiring actress whom the article had referred to. Local morticians were just as mystified, since none of the local cemeteries had power outlets located near the graves, something that would no doubt be required if a tombstone were to be equipped with an automated teller machine.

Editors at the *San Francisco Chronicle* replaced the dubious article with a message that read, "This story has been removed by SF Gate because of questions concerning its accuracy raised by the *Bozeman (Mont.) Daily Chronicle*. No death notice could be found with the name of the rancher who supposedly set up an automated teller machine at his gravesite so his family would visit."

Despite the findings of the *Bozeman Daily Chronicle,* Jenkins insisted that the story was true and explained that some of the details had been concealed to protect the grave from tourists and vandals. "I am legally constrained from fully disclosing what I know about the details, but I would argue that it is not possible to discount this story as fiction based upon the facts known by the *Bozeman Daily Chronicle* or any other news outlet," Jenkins wrote in an e-mail.

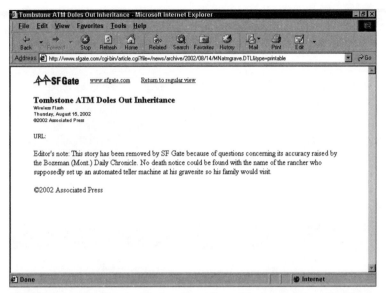

This is the message that was displayed to visitors of the San Francisco Chronicle's
*Web site after a dubious article about a cash-dispensing tombstone was removed
by the paper's editors.*

As far-fetched as this story seems, Jenkins is apparently standing
behind it and is no doubt hoping that other people will see the advantages
of "cashing out" in this unique way.

Sources: e-mail correspondence, *San Francisco Chronicle*,
Snopes.com, Wireless Flash

s Osama bin Laden recruiting Muppet characters to his cause? That was the baffling question everyone was asking in October 2001 when a bizarre picture emerged showing Bert, one of *Sesame Street*'s most recognizable characters, standing next to the world's most wanted terrorist.

THE ODD COUPLE

ANP News Agency, October 2001

This story has its origins in 1996, when a San Francisco–based Web designer named Dino Ignacio created a humorous Web site designed to prove that Bert, the yellow-skinned, spiky-haired character from the children's television show *Sesame Street,* was engaged in evil conspiracies.

"We have reason to believe that Bert of *Sesame Street* is evil and you should keep your children away from him," the site alleged. "Here in these pages are collected incriminating images and documents that prove that Bert is not the lovable harmless geek he so successfully makes us think he is."

The site was full of digitally altered pictures that showed Bert alongside notorious crooks and evil characters like Hitler, O. J. Simpson, and the Unabomber.

The original "Bert Is Evil" Web site, circa 1997.

Word of the bizarre Web site quickly spread throughout cyberspace, and people flocked to the site to see pictures of Bert in various poses with celebrities and prominent historical figures. In the years following the site's creation, dozens of duplicates and variations of the original were created on the Web. Dino's work earned praise from all corners of the globe and even garnered a "Webby Award"—the on-line equivalent to an Oscar.

The Web site was created purely for fun, and no one in his or her wildest dreams could have predicted what would happen five years later.

Fast-forward to October 2001, when the United States and other countries were avenging the September 11 terrorist attacks against the United States. On October 5 and October 9, photographers from several news services took pictures of anti-American rallies in Bangladesh.

Several of the pictures showed protesters carrying a poster featuring a collage of bin Laden pictures. Incredibly, on the right side of the poster, one of the pictures showed an angry-looking Bert standing next to Osama bin Laden.

A picture of an anti-American rally taken in Bangladesh by Angence France-Presse. Look in the bottom right-hand corner of the photograph and you will see Sesame Street's *Bert standing beside a smaller image of Osama bin Laden.*

Pictures showing the pro–bin Laden poster were circulated to newspapers and Web sites by the newswire services. Although several observant Internet users noticed Bert in the photographs, they naturally assumed someone had manipulated the photos as a prank.

Reuters, one of the news services that had taken pictures at the Bangladesh rally, began to receive queries from people looking for an explanation to this truly bizarre discovery. Why was Bert standing next to Osama bin Laden in the photograph? Was it possible that Reuters had planted Bert in the photograph as a lark? At one point, Reuters was reportedly receiving so many phone calls about the mystery photo that a picture editor jokingly began answering the phone, "Bert and Ernie hot line."

This is a smaller version of the AFP photograph. Bert is circled on the right.

Reuters denied that any doctoring had taken place and issued a statement defending their photographer: "Reuters stands by the pictures taken on October 5 and 9, 2001, by photographer Rafiqur Rahman during anti-American demonstrations in Dhaka. The pictures show posters featuring images of both Osama bin Laden and the character Bert from the U.S. children's TV show *Sesame Street.* The photograph is legitimate and has not been altered. It is against our policy to alter visual images, either still or moving, beyond the require- ments of normal image enhancement." A spokesperson for Reuters also pointed out that Rahman wasn't familiar with Bert. "The photographer is as bemused as we are," she said. "He didn't know what that furry creature was."

The other news services that had taken pictures of the protest, including the Associated Press, also denied that the photos had been altered.

The mystery deepened. How in the world did a wholesome, lovable creature such as Bert end up in a picture with the world's most wanted terrorist?

The most likely culprit seemed to be Dino Ignacio, proprietor of the original "Bert Is Evil" Web site. However, Dino denied any role in creating the picture, pointing out that although his "Bert Is Evil" Web site was still open to the public, he hadn't actively maintained it since 1998. "I had nothing to do with this," Ignacio was quoted as saying. "That image was never on my site."

So if it wasn't Dino, who was it? It seems that the picture of Bert standing next to Bin Laden was placed on the Internet by Dennis Pozniak, a Canadian, who was a fan of the original "Bert Is Evil" phenomenon and who had created a duplicate Web site with even more pictures of Bert in amusing, albeit controversial, poses. The bin Laden photo was apparently created a few years before the September 11 terrorist attacks. "No one could have been more shocked than me," the Canadian told ABCNews.com. "I never expected one of my fake photos to end up in a real news photo. It blew me away."

Dino said he had received the picture by e-mail but decided not to post it out of respect for the victims of the September 11 terrorist attacks. "This image has been e-mailed to me countless times since September 11," Dino said in a statement on his Web site on October 11, 2001. "Yesterday a lot of you alerted me to a picture of a Taliban propaganda poster with Bert! Reality is imitating the Web! I am honestly freaked out!" he wrote.

Although Dino refused to post the Bert/bin Laden picture on his own Web site, it ended up surfacing elsewhere on the Web. Once on the Web, the image was discovered by a print shop owner in Bangladesh who happened to be scouring the Internet for pictures of Osama bin Laden. The pictures were to be used in a poster he was creating.

The print shop owner downloaded the image without noticing Bert's presence and added it to his poster, which was then mass-produced and put up for sale in his shop.

In a story by the Associated Press, the owner of the print shop explained that the inclusion of Bert in the poster was completely unintentional. In fact, like the Reuters photographer, he said he didn't even know who Bert was. "We did not give the pictures a second look or realize what they signified until you pointed it out to us," he said.

For his part, Dino, the creator of the original "Bert Is Evil" Web site, decided to throw in the towel and shut down his Web site altogether shortly after pictures of Bert standing next to bin Laden began to appear on the Web.

In a notice posted on his Web site, Dino said the joke had gotten out of control, and he cited the need to protect children as the main reason he decided to shut his site down.

"My main motivation in killing the site is that I hope it helps stop the idea from germinating anymore into the mainstream. I fear that it may destroy the character's credibility with children. I cannot allow that to happen. I myself grew up on *Sesame Street* and it was an important part of my childhood."

Although the original "Bert Is Evil" Web site is now gone, other "Bert Is Evil" Web sites still live on in infamy, much to the chagrin of the producers of *Sesame Street*.

While the owners of *Sesame Street* were clearly, and understandably, incensed to discover Bert adorning a bin Laden poster, most people found humor in the fact that a children's character such as Bert could end up standing next to the world's most wanted terrorist—and in Bangladesh, of all places.

Looking at this strange turn of events another way, it is the magical power of the Internet that made it possible for Bert to make the rather bizarre leap from television celebrity to Osama bin Laden's sidekick. As one observer, Isabelle Adam, wrote on her Web site, "Even if the posters themselves are not proof of Bert's evil-mastermind right-hand-man status, they are testimony of the power of the Internet and the spreading tendrils of Western civilization. Much as anticapitalism protesters arrive at demonstrations wearing name-brand watches and footwear, unable even with such pure intent to escape the very thing they're campaigning against, so too the Bangladeshi protesters find themselves caught in the same trap. Only here, it is a children's television character serving to remind them of their being part of one global community."

Yet, if there were any positive spin to be put on Bert's newfound fame, *Sesame Street* executives didn't see it. They quickly issued a statement condemning Bert's connection to Osama bin Laden. "We're outraged that our characters would be used in this unfortunate and distasteful manner. This is not at all humorous. The people responsible for this should be ashamed of themselves," they said.

And what does Bert have to say about all of this controversy? When a Fox News reporter demanded to know where the Muppet was, a spokesperson remained tight-lipped. "No comment," she said.

Sources: ABC News, Isabelle Adam, Associated Press, Fox News, *Los Angeles Times*, official "Bert Is Evil" Web site

occer fans have a reputation for being some of the rowdiest and noisiest fans in the sporting world, and South Korea's soccer enthusiasts are no exception. So when a South Korean radio station jumped the gun in June 2002 and mistakenly reported that their national soccer team would be in the World Cup finals, sheer pandemonium broke out across the country. And it was all because of a single, erroneous mobile phone message.

KICKING UP A COMMOTION

Seoul Broadcasting System, June 2002

The confusion began on June 27, 2002, when television actress and broadcast personality Choi Hwa-Jung was in the studios of Seoul Broadcasting System's Power FM, one of South Korea's most popular radio stations. While she was on the air, she received an urgent message on her mobile phone. Glancing down at her screen, she was stunned to learn that Germany had been disqualified from the World Cup finals because at least one of its players had failed a drug test. That meant that South Korea would take Germany's place in the World Cup finals, soccer's most revered tournament.

The incredible news had been relayed to Choi by her assistant, who had in turn heard it from her friend. A jubilant Choi quickly read the bulletin on the air, causing a commotion in the radio station's control room. Station employees motioned for Choi to keep the information to herself, but the cat had already been let out of the bag. "After receiving the message from her assistant, she became too excited and read it into the microphone," said a spokesperson for the radio station who was quoted by the Agence France-Presse wire service.

As the unbelievable announcement was carried through the airwaves, excited fans rejoiced across the country and reveled in the possibility that South Korea could actually have a shot at winning the World Cup. In the city of Busan, on the southeastern tip of the Korean peninsula, hundreds of department store shoppers reportedly went into hysterics after learning about the good news. Hysterical fans also swarmed the Web site of the Korea Football Association, knocking it off-line for a period of time, and flooded the telephone lines of the KOWOC—the Korean World Cup organizing committee. To make matters worse, several popular Internet sites jumped into the fray and broke the news without checking the veracity of the report.

Alas, it was not to be. The story was determined to be false about four minutes later and Choi apologized four times on the air for broadcasting the erroneous information. The KOWOC also issued a statement denying the rumor. Their World Cup dreams shattered, scores of angry listeners deluged the radio station with telephone calls and left irate messages on the station's Web site.

After the incident, Choi's career as a radio personality seemed to be hanging by a thread. Reacting to the furor that Choi's blunder had caused, Power FM's owner discussed the possibility of punishing the station for their irresponsible actions. But in the end, Choi and her staff were spared further embarrassment, and Choi was allowed to continue her radio-hosting duties. This time, we hope, she'll keep her cell phone turned off while on the air.

Sources: Agence France-Presse, *Korea Herald, Korea Times*

> It probably wasn't the first fake byline to appear in a newspaper article, but it was almost certainly the first byline to read, "By Fake Byline."

DOES THIS MEAN THE STORY IS FAKE, TOO?

New York Times, July 1990

On July 20, 1990, an article on page A8 of the prestigious *New York Times* appeared under bold type that read, "By Fake Byline." Written under the byline in smaller type were the words "Special to *The New York Times.*"

The *New York Times* said the byline was just dummy text and that it never should have appeared in the actual newspaper. The error was caused by an inexperienced employee who neglected to remove the dummy text from the paper's computer system before the newsprint started rolling off the presses. Fortunately, the embarrassing gaffe didn't creep into all editions of the newspaper.

"The story was not supposed to have a byline on it, but our computer format doesn't work without one," said a *New York Times* spokesperson quoted by the Associated Press. "We plug in 'Fake Byline' so the format works. It's supposed to be deleted, but . . ."

Sources: Associated Press, Reuters

> Some people, it seems, learn the hard way. When student journalists at the University of Washington failed to fact-check a front-page campus newspaper article, they got more than they bargained for—and made their newspaper the laughingstock of the country.

BIG A** MISTAKE

University of Washington, October 2002

The trouble began when an inexperienced journalism student working for the University of Washington's student newspaper, the *Daily Evergreen,* was preparing an article on Filipino-American History Month. In an attempt to give the story some historical context, the reporter took some material from an Internet site called PinoyLife.com and without checking it for accuracy or citing her source, used it in her article. It ran on October 3, 2002.

The story read in part, "On Oct. 18, 1857, the first Filipinos landed on the shores of Morro Bay, California, on a Spanish galleon called the *Nuestra Señora de Buena Esperanza,* which translates to 'The Big Ass Spanish Boat.'"

Unbeknownst to the student, she had just been duped. The material she had plucked off the Internet came from an article that was meant to be humorous. The ship's correct name in English is "Our Lady of Good Hope."

The strange and laughable translation was questioned by at least one student editor, but the decision was made to keep the information in the article because it came from what appeared to be a credible Web site.

The article went to print and it ran on the front page of the campus newspaper, where the mysterious translation caught the attention of an ESL (English as a second language) specialist at the university. She wrote a letter to the editor, chastising the paper for its "vulgar" translation. She ended her letter by noting, "Never has there been a better argument for more required foreign language courses."

The paper responded with a front-page retraction and apology. For his part, the *Evergreen*'s editor in chief said he was shocked that such a gross error had slipped by under his watch. "I'm still stunned," he said in an interview with the *Seattle Times*. "It was an entire breakdown. I didn't think anything like that would ever get in the paper. We need to do a lot more proofing."

Despite the seriousness of the situation, the *Evergreen*'s staff adviser was able to see the lighter side of the paper's blunder. "A lot of the people are chuckling about it," he was quoted by the *Seattle Times* as saying, "because it's such a flagrant mistake."

Indeed, the *Evergreen*'s experience is a lesson to us all—don't believe everything you read on the Internet!

Sources: *Daily Evergreen,* PinoyLife.com, *Seattle Times*

he *New York Times* has run thousands of corrections over the years, but none so unusual and humorous as the correction they were forced to run on April 2, 2001.

SPEECHLESS IN NEW YORK

New York Times, April 2001

The previous day, the paper had run a listing in their television section for a movie called *The Sea Hawk* that was being aired on the Turner Classic Movies cable channel. It described the flick as a "high-tech swashbuckler about a mild-mannered news assistant who ransacks a New York newspaper office via remote control." The stars were listed as Tim Sastrowardoyo and Marilyn McCauley.

For those readers and videophiles who noticed the suspicious movie listing, it seemed like a strategically placed April Fools' Day joke. After all, *The Sea Hawk* was actually a film about an English nobleman. Not to mention the fact that remote control devices didn't exist in 1924, when the movie was made. Moreover, a quick check of any movie/video guide would yield no information on either of the two names listed as the film's stars—Tim Sastrowardoyo and Marilyn McCauley. That's because they were not actors at all—they actually worked for the *New York Times*.

Although it appeared as though the *New York Times* had tried to pull a fast one on their readers, it was actually the readers, not the newspaper, who had the last laugh.

An investigation by the *New York Times* revealed that the movie description was a "dummy listing" created in December 1998 when the paper was testing its movie database. The listing never got deleted and somehow got left in the database by accident, only to be retrieved three years later when *The Sea Hawk* was scheduled to air on April 1, 2001. While preparing the television listings for that particular day, *New York Times* staff pulled the description of *The Sea Hawk* from their database, unaware that the information was bogus. It was pure coincidence that the fictitious information happened to run on April Fools' Day. The mistake had never been caught before because this was the first time *The Sea Hawk* had run since the dummy listing was created.

In a correction that appeared the following day, the *New York Times* said they were "speechless" that the mistake had occurred on April Fools' Day and they regretted any inconvenience that readers had been caused as a result of the unusual gaffe.

Sources: *New York Daily News, New York Times*

> When Cheyenne, Wyoming, resident Dr. Jonathan Singer came across a strange broadcast on his satellite dish one day in 1984, he thought he might have stumbled across a top-secret military transmission. Either that, or he was in some kind of inexplicable time warp.

WELCOME TO THE TWILIGHT ZONE

ABC News, November 1984

The day was November 4, 1984, two days before the 1984 presidential election. Dr. Singer was watching a program on his satellite dish when he heard that Reagan had won the election. Singer couldn't believe his ears because the election hadn't even taken place yet. But sure enough, there were Peter Jennings and David Brinkley on his television screen, interviewing political analysts and discussing Reagan's trouncing of Walter Mondale. According to the broadcast, Reagan had swept the election in a landslide, taking 301 electoral votes to Mondale's 43.

"I couldn't believe it," Dr. Singer was quoted as saying.

I thought I was in the twilight zone. First, I looked at my watch, and then I remembered I wasn't wearing one. Then I looked at the calendar to be sure I hadn't slept through the election. The next thing I thought was that, with all the predictions and pre-polls and everything, maybe that's all there was, and there wouldn't be any election. I felt sort of cheated.

Then my mother called from Milwaukee, and I told her about it. Afterward, she called ABC, and they told her that what I'd seen had been something that I had illegally intercepted. "Unofficially," they told her, "all we can tell you is that we can't comment on it." Honestly, by the time my mother had called me again, I had the feeling I had interrupted some kind of a secret military operation.

But it was not to be. The freaky broadcast was actually a dress rehearsal that was being carried out by ABC News in preparation for their real election coverage on November 6. The practice run was being transmitted to ABC-affiliated stations across the United States, but somehow Singer's satellite dish had picked up the signal, giving him a private, unintended screening of ABC's preparations for election night.

Fortunately for ABC, they practiced the right outcome. Two days later, Reagan won the election, taking 525 electoral votes to Mondale's 13.

Source: *Parade* magazine

he major television networks are notorious for their overzealous use of public opinion polls and exit poll data when trying to predict the outcome of an election. The result is that they often slip up, awarding an election victory to the wrong person. Looking back in history, it seems that most of the embarrassing moments have occurred after the polls have closed, not before.

JUST SLIGHTLY AHEAD OF THEIR TIME

ABC News, November 1998

That wasn't the case in 1998, when ABC News created an entirely new controversy by publishing election results before people had even had a chance to vote. Talk about getting ahead of yourself!

On the evening of November 2, 1998, visitors to the Web site of ABC News were treated to a real spectacle. The news organization was boldly reporting that voters had ushered in Democrat Gray Davis as the new governor of California. That was impossible, because the polls weren't scheduled to open for another eighteen hours!

Internet users were also able to browse complete results of every U.S. Senate, House, and governor's race across the country, a baffling phenomenon considering people hadn't even voted yet. While some people may have thought for a moment that ABC News had some super-duper new technology for forecasting election results, the likelihood that this was human error quickly sunk in.

The results were up on ABC's Web site for several hours before Matt Drudge, an on-line gossip columnist, became aware of them. Drudge quickly jumped on the story and published the news on his legendary Web site, the Drudge Report. "In what will clearly go down as one of the biggest Internet mistakes of all time, ABC NEWS has suddenly started to report Election Day results—before Election Day," he wrote.

Once ABC discovered what had happened, they promptly removed the embarrassing data from their Web site. Drudge had a field day with ABC's screw-up, calling it the "biggest online nightmare of the Internet Era." He jokingly added that Thomas Dewey had been elected president and pope.

Horrified ABC News executives could only shake their heads in disbelief. "It wasn't our finest hour," admitted Michelle Bergman, manager of communications for ABCNews.com, in an interview with the Associated Press.

The following day, Bergman explained that the data had accidentally been published on the Web site during an internal test. "In anticipation of today's election, we were testing our election result Web pages and we inadvertently published those pages," she said. "We are taking steps to introduce a series of checks and balances to make sure it doesn't happen again."

A statement was also posted to the ABC News Web site. "Last night, during testing of the site (abcnews.com), we inadvertently posted results and erroneous predictions on the outcomes of the political races," the statement said. "There was no bias intended by what we posted, and the predictions do not reflect the reporting or news judgment of ABC News."

ABCNews.com: Premature Election '98 Results - Microsoft Internet Explorer

File   Edit   View   Favorites   Tools   Help   Links »

SENATE

ALABAMA

CANDIDATE	VOTE TOTAL	PERCENT
SHELBY (REP) *	392635	66%
SUDDITH (DEM)	201301	34%

% of precincts reporting: 100

ALASKA

CANDIDATE	VOTE TOTAL	PERCENT
SONNEMAN (DEM)	51232	50%
MURKOWSKI (REP) *	49207	48%
GOTTLIEB (GRN)	1136	1%
KOHLHAAS (LTN)	929	1%

% of precincts reporting: 100

ARIZONA

CANDIDATE	VOTE TOTAL	PERCENT
MCCAIN (REP) *	379141	64%
RANGER (DEM)	204852	34%
ZAJAC (LTN)	6200	1%
PARK (RFM)	5737	1%

% of precincts reporting: 100

Done   Internet

The "dummy" election results accidentally published by ABCNews.com

Later analysis of ABC's data revealed some surprising information. Incredibly, ABC's test numbers had correctly picked the winning candidate in 32 of the 36 races for governor and 29 of the 34 contests for Senate, leading some people to speculate that ABC wasn't telling the whole truth. Nevertheless, ABC News insisted the numbers were simply "dummy" numbers chosen at random for testing the system, and not derived from any special forecasting models.

The employee who caused the accident was eventually fired from ABC News, apparently in part because the person circulated a celebratory e-mail suggesting that the mistake would generate "more PR than money could ever buy."

In a strange coincidence, ABC's Web site blunder occurred on the fiftieth anniversary of the most famous newspaper gaffe of all time. On the evening of November 2, 1948, the *Chicago Tribune* prepared an erroneous headline declaring that Thomas Dewey had been elected president of the United States. (See page 180.)

Sources: Associated Press, *Atlanta Journal-Constitution,* Drudge Report, Freedom Forum, *Hollywood Reporter,* Reuters, Wired News

When it comes to open-mike gaffes on television, usually it's the host or guest who is caught making an off-color remark. It's rare to catch a producer in the act. After all, the producer is supposed to be operating behind the camera and is normally not seen or heard from by the viewing audience. Sometimes, however, a technical gaffe causes a producer's voice to be heard on the air.

BEAUTY AND THE BEAST

Canadian Broadcasting Corporation, November 2000

This is precisely what happened on November 27, 2000, as the Canadian Broadcasting Corporation (CBC), one of Canada's major television networks, was providing live coverage of Canada's federal election results. During the broadcast, a CBC television producer let his male hormones get the better of him, resulting in one of the most famous open-mike gaffes in Canadian television history.

The producer, who thought his microphone was connected to an internal audio feed only, was heard saying, "This is Logan Day's wife.

I've never met her, but apparently she's got tits that'd stop a—" His comment was interrupted by a CBC technician who pulled the plug on the transmission as soon as he realized it was being broadcast live. Logan Day was the son of Stockwell Day, who at the time was leader of one of Canada's major political parties, the Canadian Alliance Party. Logan's wife, Juliana Thiessen Day, was a former beauty queen.

The outrageous remark was heard across the province of British Columbia on Canada's CTV television network, which was using a feed provided by the CBC, and complaints began to pour in almost immediately from irate viewers. Shortly after CBC executives learned of the incident, they faxed a formal apology to Stockwell Day and his daughter-in-law. An apology was also read on the air. Disciplinary action was taken against the unnamed producer a few days later, and he was suspended for ten days without pay.

If you are wondering how the producer's sentence ended, you're not alone. Mordecai Richler, one of Canada's most celebrated novelists, said that the "tantalizingly incomplete sentence" kept him awake for several nights as he tried to complete it. He was later informed by a source deep within the CBC that the producer's utterance was "tits that'd stop a train."

Sources: Canadian Press, *National Post*

ave you ever wanted to sink into a corner after saying something really stupid? Well, imagine being a television anchor. When a broadcaster makes an embarrassing gaffe on the air, the entire viewing audience gets to see it. Although some on-air mistakes are relatively harmless, others can haunt a television anchor for the rest of his or her career.

A NEW WAY TO GET A WHITE BALANCE

Channel 10, Brisbane, Queensland, Australia, June 2000

ne of the more embarrassing slipups I've ever come across happened to Marie-Louise Theile, a news anchor at Channel 10 in Brisbane, Queensland, Australia. Following a commercial break on the station's June 22, 2000, broadcast, the camera cut to Theile and her coanchor, Geoff Mullins, who were in the middle of a lively conversation.

With thousands of people watching in their living rooms, Theile began whining about her husband, a high-profile plastic surgeon. According to the *Courier Mail,* she said, ". . . but this arsehole I'm married to, he goes, 'Oh, I want to go skiing,' oh, okay, I wanna go to Europe, oh, okay . . ."

Suddenly, it dawned on the two anchors that their conversation was being broadcast live on the air. Realizing that she had just aired her dirty laundry in public, Theile went white as a sheet and looked to the side of the screen in shock. Mullins, who was also visibly shaken, quickly switched to a weather report while Theile tried to regain her composure. The whole incident lasted about nine seconds, but for Theile, it must have seemed like an eternity.

Stunned by what had just happened, the station immediately went into damage-control mode, convening an emergency meeting of its management team to decide how to respond to the gaffe.

Later, the station issued a statement defending Theile. "It was a lighthearted conversation taking place off air," the statement said. "Unfortunately, due to an operation error, parts of the conversation were broadcast. We regret that that happened. The matter has been dealt with and there will be no further comment."

The following day, Theile issued an on-air apology and tried to set the record straight about her apparently stormy marriage:

"Well, last night a part of a conversation taking place here in the studio during a commercial break was broadcast to air. The conversation was lighthearted, it was in no way meant seriously. My husband, David, and I have a truly wonderful relationship and I'm very sorry that the comments went to air, and I regret any offense that viewers may have taken from them."

An investigation later revealed that the mishap was partly caused by an internal communications glitch. A technician at the station pressed the wrong intercom button and failed to notify the two anchors that they would be returning to the air in ten seconds.

While Theile succeeded in embarrassing both herself and her husband, she also managed to make Australian broadcasting history. A newspaper columnist in Sydney included Theile's goof in his list of Australia's "top twenty greatest moments in small screen embarrassment."

Sources: Australian Broadcasting Corporation,
Courier Mail (Brisbane), *Daily Telegraph* (Sydney), *Sun Herald* (Sydney),
Sunday Mail (Queensland, Australia)

The late 1960s will always be remembered as the time when man first set foot on the moon. They'll also be remembered for the greatest television-programming blunder of all time.

HEIDI'S INTERCEPTION

NBC Television Network, November 1968

On November 17, 1968, the American Football League's New York Jets were playing the Oakland Raiders in a highly anticipated and exciting game. Two of the game's greatest quarterbacks, Joe Namath of the Jets and Daryle Lamonica of the Raiders, were going head-to-head in what would likely be a fierce and very intense showdown.

The game got under way at 4 P.M. and it was as exhilarating as everyone had hoped it would be. Toward the end of the fourth quarter, the Jets were tied with the Raiders 29–29. Then, with just over a minute to go, Jim Turner of the Jets booted a field goal from the twenty-six-yard line, putting his team ahead 32–29. There were now only sixty-five seconds to play, and fans were on the edge of their seats. But many fans thought the game was over. After all, did anyone really expect the Raiders to score with only a minute remaining in the game?

It was now 6:59 P.M. NBC had previously scheduled the children's movie *Heidi* to air at that time and the network was faced with a difficult dilemma. Should they continue with their coverage of the football game or adhere to their original schedule and run *Heidi*?

In the minutes leading up to 7 P.M., thousands of television viewers clogged the NBC switchboard, asking whether the game would continue until the end, or whether *Heidi* would air on time.

Dick Cline, who was NBC's broadcast operations supervisor at the time, was waiting for a call from NBC executives to let him know what he should do. "I knew the executives in sports were trying to get permission to keep the game on," Cline was quoted by the *Chicago Tribune* as saying. "I knew they were going to try to call me if they got permission."

But Cline never got the call, and he decided to pull the football game off the air. Without any warning or notice to the millions of football fans who were glued to their television sets, much of the network suddenly cut to the movie, giving Heidi one of the greatest interceptions in NFL history.

What Cline didn't realize was that NBC executives had received permission to keep the game on the air and they had been trying to reach him. But because the phone lines were jammed with callers inquiring about the fate of *Heidi,* they were unable to get through.

After the football game had been taken off the air, NBC president Julian Goodman managed to reach Cline on a separate telephone circuit and told him to reinstate the game. But it was too late. In 1968, national television broadcasts were distributed over telephone lines, not through satellite like they are today. In order to get the football game back on the air, Cline needed to get in touch with the appropriate telephone company authorities. But he wasn't able to reach the right people in time.

Meanwhile, in homes across America, viewers were stunned. How could NBC stop the broadcast at such a crucial point in the game? Thousands of irate fans jammed the already overloaded NBC switchboard in protest, but it was to no avail. As syndicated columnist Art Buchwald once observed, "Men who wouldn't get out of their chairs during an earthquake rushed to the phones to scream obscenities." Millions of angry viewers walked away from their sets that day, and most assumed that the Jets had triumphed. But as luck would have it, the final minute of the game saw a complete turnaround in the score.

As it turned out, the last sixty seconds of play had an ending that one would expect to see only in a Hollywood movie. Raiders quarterback Daryle Lamonica threw a pass to Charlie Smith, who sprinted past Jets rookie Mike D'Amato to catch the ball and score a touchdown. The Raiders kicked an extra point and were now ahead 36–32. What happened next was unbelievable. The Jets fumbled the kickoff and it was recovered at the two-yard line by Preston Ridlehuber of the Raiders, who ran it into the end zone for another touchdown. In an astonishing reversal, the Raiders ended up winning the game 43–32.

It was an incredible finish, but virtually the only people who had witnessed it were the fans in the stadium. With *Heidi* now running on most of their stations, NBC ran a ticker along the bottom of the movie alerting fans to the final score. Nobody could believe their eyes. The Raiders had scored two touchdowns in the final minute of the game and NBC viewers had missed the whole thing? Fans were incensed and they descended on NBC's switchboard like an angry mob of linebackers.

The tidal wave of calls that evening had actually crashed the phone exchange at NBC's Manhattan offices at Rockefeller Plaza and when viewers couldn't get through to NBC, they flooded the New York Police Department, the New York Telephone Company, and the *New York Times* with calls. After tens of thousands of protest calls had been logged, NBC was forced to make an apology. Julian Goodman, the president of NBC, issued the following statement shortly after the game ended: "It was a forgivable error committed by humans who were concerned about the children who expected to see *Heidi* at 7 P.M. I missed the game as much as anyone else."

So why didn't Cline use common sense and keep the game on the air for another few minutes? NBC policy at the time dictated that the network must honor their commitments to advertisers. NBC had sold the 7 P.M.–9 P.M. slot to Timex and so Cline technically made the right decision—at least as far as his job was concerned. He said he would have lost his job had he decided to preempt *Heidi* in favor of the ball game.

"I was saved by the set of conditions [distributed to network executives each week]," Cline said in an interview published by the NFL. "I had it in print. In fact, the vice president of my division told me that if I had taken it on my own and stayed with the game, I would have been fired."

"The *Heidi* game," as it is now known, had two immediate impacts on the broadcasting world. The NFL changed their television contracts to require networks to show football games in their entirety. Incomplete telecasts would no longer be tolerated.

And on a more amusing note, NBC reinstalled a phone in their broadcast-operation control room that was wired to a separate telephone exchange. The phone had originally been installed so that NBC executives could get through to the control room in case of an emergency. It had been removed a few weeks prior to the *Heidi* incident because NBC employees were using the line to make personal calls. But the phone was temporarily brought back after the programming debacle and appropriately called "the *Heidi* phone"—named after the notorious game that promptly brought the phone back into service.

They say that time heals all wounds. Although it's now more than thirty years later, many football fans have yet to forgive NBC for their memorable blunder in 1968.

Sources: *Chicago Tribune*, Footballology.com, *Los Angeles Times*, National Football League, NBC Sports, other news sources, Raiders.com, Real Change News

You never know what you're going to see on the evening news. That was certainly true on January 22, 1991, when viewers were treated to a rather rare spectacle on the set of the *CBS Evening News* with Dan Rather. At 6:30 P.M. EST, as millions of Americans tuned in to watch the veteran journalist begin his live news broadcast, a group of AIDS activists who opposed the Gulf War burst onto the set, startling Rather and the rest of his crew.

ACTING UP

CBS Evening News, January 1991

The protesters, members of an AIDS activist group called ACT UP (AIDS Coalition to Unleash Power), began chanting, "Fight AIDS, not Arabs! Fight AIDS, not Arabs!" It was certainly an amusing sight for television viewers to behold, as the face of one of the protesters appeared in the left-hand corner of the screen, only to be quickly yanked off the set by the crew. As CBS employees looked on in disbelief from the newsroom behind the anchor desk, Rather quickly cut to a commercial, telling viewers, "We're going to take a break for a commercial just now. . . . We'll break for a commercial, thank you very much."

However, no commercial appeared and the screen went black. Several seconds later, the sound came back on and viewers could hear a commotion in the background as the protesters were forcibly removed from the set. Rather's face then reappeared on the screen and he apologized to audiences for the interruption. "We're sorry about that . . . had a bit of an eruption here in the broadcast. We're going to take things right from the top."

Rather then regained his composure and continued on with the newscast. Later in the show, he issued yet another apology to viewers. "I want to apologize to you for the way the broadcast came on the air tonight. There were some rude people here. They tried to stage a demonstration. They've been ejected from the studio but our apologies for the way we began our coverage of the Gulf War."

John Weir, one of the protesters that day, explained in an interview on National Public Radio how the group managed to elude CBS's apparently lax security:

> **My group had planned to take NBC News and CBS News and, let's see . . . I guess we never got into ABC and we never got into NBC, but we did get into the *CBS Nightly News* with**

Dan Rather. And the three of us went into the studios, way way west on Fifty-seventh Street, the CBS studios. And we walked down the hall. It was in the middle of the war in the Gulf and there were all of these people around. It was quite a mad scene. And they didn't even notice us trying to look like television executives. And we strolled down the hall with our fake IDs and stood by the side and waited for the show to start. And as soon as Dan Rather said "Good evening," Dale and Daryl and I ran onto the set and in front of the camera.

The protesters were promptly arrested, but they succeeded in making history, albeit in a very controversial way. The AIDS protest marked the first time in the history of the *CBS Evening News* that Dan Rather's broadcast had to cut to black because of a political protest.

Sources: CBS News, National Public Radio

> Eddie Fogler, a former NCAA coach, will go down in history as the first person to make a major blunder on a live telestrator—the device sports announcers use to illustrate plays on the television screen.

THIS AIN'T NO ETCH A SKETCH

CBS Sports, March 2002

In March 2002, Fogler was working with fellow analyst Tim Brando, preparing to do on-air commentary for an NCAA basketball game between the Georgia Bulldogs and the Southern Illinois Salukis. It was one of Fogler's first telecasts as an analyst and he slipped up big time. During a commercial break in the first half when Fogler thought the telestrator wasn't live, he drew a circle around James Hayes, the father of Bulldogs players Jarvis Hayes and Jonas Hayes, and scrawled a profanity.

Although Fogler's illustration could not be seen by the national television audience watching the game, it was visible on the monitors throughout the United Center Stadium in Chicago and to people who were watching the game via satellite.

Brando said that as soon as he saw what Fogler had written on the screen, he wiped it off. By then, however, the words had been up for five seconds, long enough for lots of people to have noticed. Fogler's stomach sank to his toes when he realized that his profane comments had been broadcast across the stadium. Brando said that Fogler was "shell-shocked" at what he had just done.

The profanity was in reference to a private discussion that the two analysts had been having about the two Hayes brothers, Jarvis and Jonas, who were playing for the University of Georgia. Brando said they had planned on focusing on the two brothers during the game and introducing them to the television audience.

The twin brothers may not have been well known to viewers, but Fogler knew them all too well. Both brothers had moved to the University of Georgia from Western Carolina University during the 1999–2000 season, when Fogler was coaching for the University of South Carolina. James Hayes hadn't called Fogler to let him know his sons wanted to change teams, and Fogler was reportedly miffed that he hadn't been given a chance to sign the two star players.

Brando had been kidding Fogler about the incident before the Georgia–Southern Illinois game. "Part of my job is to loosen up the analyst with some light banter," Brando told *The State,* a daily newspaper in Columbia, South Carolina. "So I started kidding Fogler about it before the game. I said, 'Eddie, there's no way they would have come and played for you. Everyone knew it was your last year at South Carolina. And everybody knows you're an (expletive).'"

Midway through the first half of the game, the two analysts were getting ready to talk about the Hayes brothers. "Around the middle of the first half during a commercial break, the producer told us he had found the Hayes family in the stands and was going to isolate on them. He asked Eddie to draw a circle around them," Brando told *The State*. At that moment, Fogler reportedly wrote the words "[ ] Me" near James Hayes's picture on the telestrator.

When the broadcast resumed, Fogler tried to recover from his blunder, praising James Hayes and his wife, Yvonne. He also apologized to James Hayes after the game and explained that the words had been directed at himself, not at Mr. Hayes.

Brando said he and a producer were partly responsible for what happened, since Fogler was just learning the ropes. "Anyone who has been in this business awhile knows that even when you're off the air (during a commercial), you're not really off."

Sources: *Milwaukee Journal Sentinel, State* (Columbia, South Carolina)

PART 6

GOVERNMENT GLITCHES, GOOFS, AND GAGS

ormally, emergency calls come into fire or police departments, not into the U.S. Bureau of Labor Statistics. But in November 1998, a market analyst really shook things up when he called the bureau and said he had an "extreme emergency." This type of call was anything but routine, and the situation at hand was anything but ordinary.

THE EARLY BIRD GETS THE PROFITS

U.S. Bureau of Labor Statistics, November 1998

ore on that in a moment but, first, a bit of background. Every month, the U.S. Bureau of Labor Statistics releases an employment report detailing the number of new jobs created the previous month.

Since this information reflects the overall health of the U.S. economy, the release of the employment numbers usually affects the stock and bond markets.

With billions of investment dollars on the line, the Bureau of Labor Statistics takes extreme precautions to ensure that no one has an unfair advantage in reporting the employment numbers.

Every month on a prescribed date, reporters from print and broadcast news outlets gather in a locked room at the bureau's offices at 8 A.M. in order to receive an advance peek at the employment report. At 8:30 A.M. sharp, the door is unlocked and journalists are free to report on the news.

On November 9, 1998, the day before the scheduled release of October's employment report, Ray Stone, a market analyst at Stone & McCarthy Research Associates, was reviewing data on the bureau's Web site when he noticed that an integral part of the employment report— the number of additions to nonfarm payrolls in October—had already been posted. According to the Web site, there had been an increase in employers' payrolls of 116,000 jobs in October.

Stunned by what he had just seen, Stone told his colleagues what he had just found. "He muttered something about, 'I think I have the October payroll numbers.' We thought he was crazy," said Dana Saporta, an economist at Stone & McCarthy, in an interview with the *Chicago Tribune.*

At about 9:15 A.M. EST, Stone called the bureau and attempted to reach a senior official. "He said it was an extreme emergency," Saporta explained.

Stone reached a midlevel staffer and said he would wait five minutes for the agency either to release the data officially or call back and ask him to keep quiet about his discovery.

Not knowing if anyone other than himself had seen the leaked information, and not wanting anyone to have an unfair advantage in the market, Stone posted the findings on his firm's Web site and announced the data on Bloomberg at around 9:22 A.M. Stone also e-mailed the payroll numbers to thousands of his clients, primarily institutional bond traders and portfolio managers, cautioning everyone that he couldn't be sure the numbers were legitimate.

The unexpected release of the data by Stone sent stock and bond prices higher as investors took advantage of the leaked information.

It turned out that the numbers *were* real. Now that the so-called "mother of all economic statistics" had hit the street prematurely, the bureau felt it had no choice but to officially release the full employment report a day early, and it did so at around 1:22 P.M. that day—an unprecedented decision for the bureau.

Initially, the bureau had no idea how the payroll numbers had leaked onto its Web site a full day early. "The integrity of the Bureau of Labor Statistics numbers is our top priority," said Labor Secretary Alexis Herman to reporters. "We are uncertain at this time how some data from the October report made its way to our Internet page."

It wasn't long, however, before the mystery was solved. An investigation revealed that an employee had placed the data on an internal computer server—without realizing that the computer would automatically load the information onto the agency's public Web site.

The bureau immediately promised that steps were being taken to prevent a repeat of the incident.

Commenting to the *Chicago Tribune,* Dana Saporta from Stone & McCarthy said, "It's one of those freaky things. It will probably never happen again."

Ironically, a similar incident *did* occur less than three months later. On January 12, 1999, the bureau's Producer Price Indexes (PPIs) for December were accidentally posted on the Web site a day early. This time, the computer software that controls when PPI data get released was prematurely put into production, causing the data to be posted to the bureau's public Web site.

Sources: Associated Press, *Chicago Tribune,* CNN, *Government Computer News,* Reuters, *Wall Street Journal*

Have you ever wondered how your neighbor can afford that nice car you've seen him driving? Or where he got the money for that big home-renovation project he's been undertaking? Of course, your neighbor's salary is none of your business, especially in France, where asking someone about his or her income is considered strictly taboo.

A TAXING SITUATION

French Finance Ministry, September 2001

So you can imagine the outrage that resulted in France when a computer glitch there caused thousands of people to receive private tax details that were intended for their neighbors. The glitch was discovered in September 2001 and the country's gossip mill immediately went into overdrive as residents discovered the salaries of people in their community.

Thierry Mandon, the mayor of Ris-Orangis, a town about twelve miles south of Paris, said his phone line was burning up with calls from irate taxpayers. "This is very serious," the Agence France-Presse news service quoted him as saying. "One of my employees informed me he'd received my tax statement. Another local resident who was sent a doctor's tax bill has been going around complaining about how much the doctor earned."

"It's a huge scandal—I know everything about my neighbors now," said one woman to the French newspaper *Le Parisien*. Another resident interviewed by *Le Parisien* told the newspaper she was shocked to discover her neighbor's real age. "I found out my neighbor had lied to me about her age," she said. "It turns out she's actually older than her husband. . . . I'm going to feel so uncomfortable when I bump into my neighbors from now on."

Bewildered residents flooded government offices with calls, wondering what they should do with the misdirected statements. In some French villages and towns, neighbors got together to exchange each other's tax information.

"In my twenty-five years on the job, I have never seen anything like it," said Pierre-Marie Lemoine, who worked for a government phone service set up to help people with tax questions.

Although the statements had the right name and address printed on the first page, the inside pages contained confidential tax details belonging to someone else. The problem was traced back to a computer snafu at the company that prepared the mailings. The glitch was quickly fixed and all the affected taxpayers were promised a letter of apology from France's Finance Ministry.

Sources: Agence France-Presse, Associated Press, *Daily Telegraph, Financial Times,* Reuters

ere's a warning to meeting and event planners everywhere—the Yes Men are out to get you. If you haven't heard of the Yes Men, you're not alone. This loose-knit group of anti-free-trade crusaders has a low profile, but they're rapidly gaining a worldwide reputation for their uncanny ability to impersonate employees of the World Trade Organization. In the summer of 2000, this mischievous group of pranksters pulled off one of their most elaborate and impressive hoaxes ever, proving that everything is not always as it seems on the Web.

TRICKS OF THE TRADE

World Trade Organization, August 2000

The hoax got under way in August 2000, when the Center for International Legal Studies (CILS) in Austria visited what they thought was the Web site of the World Trade Organization (WTO).

Using an e-mail address found on the Web site, the center contacted the WTO and asked if Mike Moore, the World Trade Organization's director-general, could speak at an upcoming legal seminar on international trade in Salzburg, Austria. A copy of the original e-mail is reprinted below:

BY EMAIL ONLY
Mike Moore
Director General
World Trade Organization (WTO)
Geneva, SWITZERLAND

Re: Conference on International Services
Session on International Trade
Center for International Legal Studies
Salzburg, Austria, October 26-29, 2000

Dear Mr. Moore:

I write on behalf of Professor Dennis Campbell, Director, Center for International Legal Studies ("the CILS"), Salzburg, Austria. More information about the CILS can be found on the internet at www.cils.org.

In cooperation with the American Bar Association Section of International Law and Practice and the John Marshall Law School of Chicago, Illinois, the CILS is hosting a Conference on International Services in Salzburg on October 26–29, 2000. A special session on International Trade is planned. As sub-chair of this session, I am looking for four or five speakers and a panel moderator. There are usually 60 to 80 partici-pants at these conferences. Speakers and moderators receive a substantial discount on accommodation and meals

at the conference's five-star hotel in Salzburg plus a substantial discount on the conference fee. Accompanying significant others also receive a substantial discount on accommodation and meals.

Would you be interested in serving as a speaker at or as the moderator of the Session on International Trade? If so, if you would kindly contact me at the email address as above listed or at my London chambers' address, telephone, or fax also as above listed, then I will inform Professor Campbell of your interest and he can provide you with more specific details.

Thank you for your time and consideration.

Sincerely yours,

MICHAEL BUXTON DEVINE, LL.M.
Attorney-at-Law & Barrister-at-Law
Des Moines, New York, London

/s/ Michael B. Devine

Michael B. Devine

In response to their inquiry, CILS heard back from Mike Moore directly. He was grateful for the invitation but said he might not be able to attend the conference personally—could the WTO send someone else in his place? CILS agreed to use a substitute speaker, and they subsequently received an e-mail from Alice Foley, Mike Moore's assistant, who recommended a man by the name of "Dr. Andreas Bichlbauer."

A few days later, the center received a fax from Dr. Bichlbauer confirming that he would attend the conference and speak on the subject "Trade Regulation Relaxation and Concepts of Incremental Improvement: Governing Perspectives from 1790 to the Present" [although conference organizers erroneously thought he meant "1970 to the Present"].

Unbeknownst to the Center for International Legal Studies, Dr. Bichlbauer didn't actually exist! All of this time, they had been corresponding

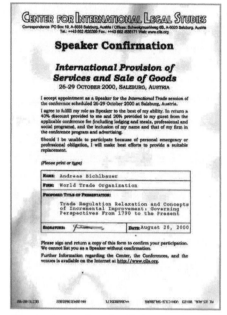

The speaker confirmation that was sent to the Center for International Legal Studies by the fictitious Andreas Bichlbauer.

with the Yes Men, who had been posing as Dr. Bichlbauer as well as Mike Moore and Alice Foley, Moore's secretary.

The seminar organizers at the CILS had been duped by a bogus Web site set up to look like the official Web site of the World Trade Organization. The deception was also facilitated by the impostor Web site's seemingly legitimate address—gatt.org. GATT (General Agreement on Tariffs and Trade) was the predecessor to the World Trade Organization.

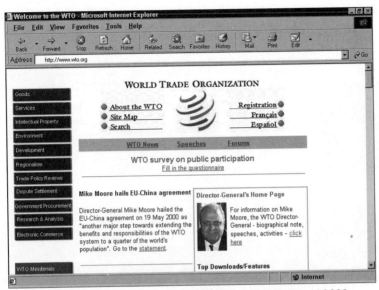

What the official World Trade Organization Web site looked like in mid-2000.

The seminar organizers had no clue they were being deceived, and they proceeded to put the fictitious Dr. Bichlbauer on the conference agenda. That started in motion an utterly comical series of events.

Accompanied by two "security assistants," the fictitious "Dr. Bichlbauer" traveled to the conference and gave a bizarre speech that stunned the conference delegates. He offered some rather preposterous suggestions during his presentation and even floated the idea that the United States should auction off the presidency to the highest bidder.

Puzzled about what they had just witnessed, the CILS fired off an e-mail to the World Trade Organization. They also requested confirmation of a rumor they had heard that Dr. Bichlbauer had been hit with a pie following his speech at the conference.

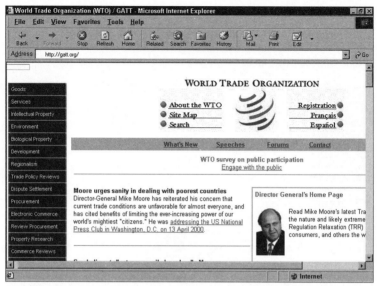

The "fake" World Trade Organization Web site created by the Yes Men, as it looked in June 2000.

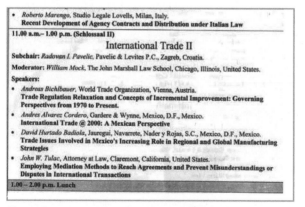

The conference agenda published by the Center for International Legal Studies, featuring Dr. Bichlbauer as a speaker.

Here is a copy of the e-mail sent by the Center for International Legal Studies to the World Trade Organization:

Date: Sat, 28 Oct 2000 04:25:28 -0400
From: Dennis Campbell
To: Alice Foley
Subject: WTO representative

Dear Ms Foley:

We were somewhat puzzled by Dr Bichlbauer's participation at the conference.

He was accompanied by someone we took to be a driver and/or security person and someone who filmed his remarks. The essential thrust of his speech appeared to be that Italians have a lesser work ethic than the Dutch, that Americans would be better off auctioning their votes in the Presidential election to the highest bidder, and that the primary role of the WTO was to create a one-world culture.

In the late afternoon, a cameraman (I think it was the same one who filmed Dr Bichlbauer's speech) appeared at the hotel and sought to interview our delegates. He said Dr Bichlbauer had been hit in the face with a pie outside the hotel and wanted to know if the delegates thought Dr Bichlbauer's speech had provoked the attack.

I have no idea whether or not Dr Bichlbauer was hit with a pie. Certainly there was no public announcement whatsoever that a WTO representative would be with us, and the meeting itself was not open to the public. Nor was the conference schedule or list of participants available to the public.

Several of our delegates (including work-ethic-impaired Italians) approached me to express concern about the speech, the alleged pie incident, and the cameraman who sought interviews in the late afternoon.

Your clarification will be appreciated.

Regards, Dennis Campbell
Center for International Legal Studies

Of course, this e-mail did not go to the real World Trade Organization. The Center for International Legal Studies was continuing to correspond with the contacts that had come from the fake Web site, so all the e-mail correspondence was going to the Yes Men, the group pulling the prank.

The Yes Men quickly replied to the seminar organizers, pretending to be Alice Foley, secretary to the director-general of the World Trade Organization:

Date: Sat, 28 Oct 2000 07:01:00 -0400
From: Alice Foley
To: Dennis Campbell
Subject: Re: WTO representative

Dear Mr. Campbell,

Indeed you are correct, Dr. Bichlbauer was in fact "pied" after speaking at the Salzburg CILS conference. At present we are not completely certain of all the details, but it appears that the cameraman you mention had something to do with it. Dr. Bichlbauer was assigned one official assistant, Ravi Bhaticharaya. Bhaticharaya did not follow proper security protocols in bringing on this cameraman, who seems to have essentially been an agent provocateur who planned the pieing from the start. And we have received one other report linking the "reporter" with this fellow.

I can express our sincere regrets in regards to this matter, and can assure you that Mr. Bhaticharaya's actions will be scrutinized over the next days with the greatest care. We hope you understand that this sort of incident reflects primarily the unfortunate circumstances under which the WTO must accomplish its work, and that our security can never be entirely adequate to the situations we face.

Please also let me know whether I may forward your e-mail to parties relevant to the investigation of this matter. And please send us any more details about this incident so that we may pursue our investigation.

As for concerns regarding Dr. Bichlbauer's talk, please be assured that we are certain he did not mean to offend with any remarks. If any parties were indeed offended, please have them write to me with their concerns, and they will be dealt with appropriately.

Best wishes,
Alice Foley, Administrative Assistant to Mike Moore

A series of entertaining e-mail exchanges followed. On November 1, the Yes Men decided to take the prank even further. They e-mailed one of the seminar organizers and informed him that Dr. Bichlbauer had contracted a "serious infection from the pie" that had been thrown at him following his speech at the conference.

Date: Wed, 1 Nov 2000 22:04:37 -0500
From: Alice Foley
To: Dennis Campbell
Subject: Investigation

Dear Professor Campbell,

Mike Moore has asked me to write you regarding the incident following Andreas Bichlbauer's lecture in Salzburg. The situation has, I regret to say, somewhat deteriorated from an already unpleasant state of affairs: Dr. Bichlbauer has contracted a rather serious infection from the pie, which forensic analysis shows contained an active bacillus agent. It is not certain whether foul play was involved. His prognosis is good.

Now that this incident has escalated to the level of a potentially much more serious crime, we must urge you to relay to us any and all information you may have regarding the circumstances of the event, and ask others who might have been present to do so as well. I know that this question will sound harsh, but could any of the lawyers present have been angry enough at Dr. Bichlbauer's lecture to do this?

We sincerely hope that some information presents itself in the coming days; besides the matter of the police inquiry, with which we are cooperating to the fullest, it is important to us to know who our enemies are, especially when they are prone to resort to such disturbing tactics.

Yours,
Alice Foley, Administrative Assistant to Mike Moore

The Yes Men weren't content to let the prank rest there. Several weeks later, after exchanging some hilarious e-mail messages with conference delegates regarding the pie-throwing incident, the Yes Men sent an e-mail to all the conference participants to inform them that Dr. Bichlbauer had died from the pie infection.

Date: Mon, 27 Nov 2000 18:13:07 -0500
From: Walther Funk
To: CILS conference delegates:
Subject: Unpleasant announcement,
URGENT REQUEST

Dear Delegates,

We apologize for interrupting your holiday season with this most unpleasant announcement.

Dr. Andreas Bichlbauer, who spoke on behalf of the WTO at the CILS conference in Salzburg on Oct. 27, and with whom many of you shared a pleasurable moment or two, has passed on. He succumbed yesterday, at 16:50 CET, to an infection thought to have been caught from the rotten pie which was hurled in his face after his Oct. 27 lecture.

We feel sure that you understand the urgency now with which we ask you all to furnish us with any and all information you may have regarding this crime, which to this day remains wholly unsolved. Our only current lead is the "voter fraud" angle. Apparently Dr. Bichlbauer said something in his talk that enraged one of the delegates, so much so that said delegate has refused to speak with us, and has accused the WTO of "encouraging voter fraud."

"Encouraging voter fraud" is furthest from our wishes, of course, and we would like to hear from others who may have heard any statements by Dr. Bichlbauer that could have been thus misconstrued. Until this subject is resolved we must proceed in the broadest possible manner.

Of course, we do thank those who replied to my colleague Werner Daitz with valuable thoughts and facts, but we are still seeking this crucial bit of information and will appreciate all responses greatly.

A memorial service for Dr. Bichlbauer will take place at the Church of St. Ruprecht at Morzinplatz in Vienna next Sunday at 4 p.m. All those who cannot attend may mail condolences here.

As you can surely understand, we ask that you keep this matter from the press's attention.

Yours until next time,
Walther Funk, Investigative Services

On November 29, almost four months after the prank began, the seminar organizers finally realized that they had been the victims of an elaborate hoax. They sent a congratulatory e-mail to Werner Daitz, one of the many WTO personas that had been created by the Yes Men.

Date: Wed, 29 Nov 2000 10:24:56 +0100
From: Christian Campbell
To: info@gatt.org
Subject: Bichlbauer R.I.P.

Dear Mr. Daitz,

Let me congratulate you and your colleagues on a well thought out and well executed prank. But since we all know that it was a joke and we know who you really are, why don't you and your friends let it rest. The joke is not so funny in the second, third, fourth . . . telling. By letting Dr. Bichlbauer R.I.P., you can devote your creative capacity and organisational skills to new objectives.

Best regards,

Christian Campbell
Center for International Legal Studies

And what did the *real* WTO have to say about being successfully impersonated by a group of anti-free-trade activists?

According to a WTO spokesperson cited by the *New York Times,* the WTO "deplored" the Yes Men's deceptive tactics but said they nonetheless respected the right of free speech on the Internet.

The Yes Men, you can be sure, are hard at work plotting their next hoax on yet another unsuspecting victim. Watch out—you could be next!

Sources: *Dollars and Sense, New York Times,* theyesmen.org

any strange objects have popped up on eBay's auction Web site over the years—a human kidney, a California high school (complete with teachers), and a sealed can of air, to name just a few. But only once has a top-secret spy plane ever graced the virtual pages of the on-line auctioneer.

"DO I GET FREE SHIPPING WITH THAT?"

WFLZ Radio, Tampa, Florida, April 2001

In April 2001, the United States was involved in a major international incident over a spy plane that had been forced to make an emergency landing in the Chinese province of Hainan Island. The plane contained sensitive U.S. military secrets and the United States wanted the plane back. The Chinese were refusing to cooperate.

While high-level diplomatic talks continued between the United States and China to get the plane back, staffers at the *MJ Morning Show*—a popular morning radio program at Tampa Bay–based WFLZ— decided to put the $80 million plane up for auction on eBay as a joke.

Using broken English and the fictitious seller name of "chingchongwo," the staffers submitted the auction to eBay at around 5:15 A.M. Pacific time on Wednesday, April 18, and pretended they were acting on behalf of the Chinese military.

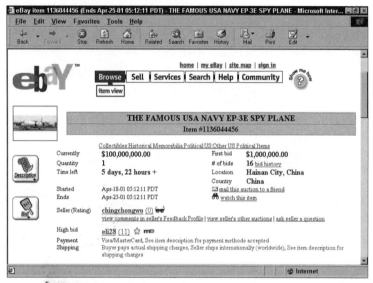

The actual "spy plane" listing that appeared on eBay.

"This is USA spy plane that was in collision with my country Chinese jet fighter," the auction listing read. "I part of the Chinese Military and have complete control over plane. The buyer of plane responsible for picking up plane. There is no sensative [sic] information on plane . . . it has all been taken off by my peoples. Nose of plane broken . . . prop be mess up also. . . . Some electronics missing and othber [sic] be smashed. You by [sic] plane as is!!!"

Bidders were instructed that the winner would have to come to China to pick up the plane, but that evidently didn't deter anyone. The first bid

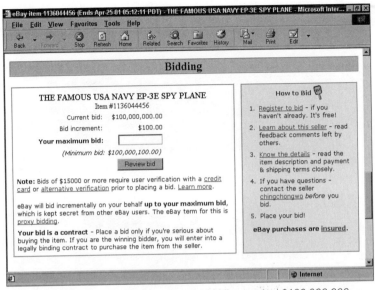

A page from the spy plane auction when the bidding reached $100,000,000.

wasn't placed until nearly twenty-four hours after the auction began, but soon bidders began tripping over themselves for the bragging rights to the plane.

By 7:30 A.M. Pacific time on Wednesday, the bidding had reached a whopping $100 million. Around that time, eBay became aware of the prank and quickly pulled the plug on the auction—more than twenty-four hours after the stunt had begun.

Staff at the morning show were amused that the prank auction had lasted so long. M. J. Kelly, a deejay at the station, said eBay needed to get a sense of humor. "They need to just laugh at this stuff," he said in an interview with *Tech-TV*.

Sources: ABCNews.com, CNN, eBay, *St. Petersburg Times, Santa Cruz Sentinel,* Tech-TV

> f you ever get the urge to create a Web site about North Korea, it would be wise to recall what happened to David Burgess, a former political science student at the University of Saskatchewan in Canada.

SPY GAME

Government of North Korea, June 1996

Following a school trip to North Korea in 1995, Burgess decided to create a Web site with pamphlets he had obtained during his travels to the secretive Communist nation. It sounds innocent enough, but the South Korean government thought otherwise. It publicly declared Burgess a subversive, and within days the bewildered political science major found himself embroiled in a cyber firestorm between North and South Korea, the likes of which the world had never seen before. All because of a Web site. The controversy erupted in 1996, the year after Burgess launched his site.

Burgess's on-line activities had come to the attention of *Chungang Ilbo,* a South Korean newspaper, which wrote an article strongly condemning the site. "Teens and college students who are exposed to the site may blindly accept the North Korean idea," the article argued.

"Steps to prevent ideological pollution are urgently required." The article insinuated that Burgess's Web site was possibly supported by North Korea.

That article tipped off the South Korean authorities about Burgess's site, and they wasted no time issuing an order to their citizens. The two Koreas had been enemies since the Korean War ended in 1953, and the South Korean government feared that North Korea was beginning to use the Internet to spread propaganda.

Invoking Chapter 2, Article 7, of South Korea's National Security Law, which laid out strict penalties for people who associated with anti-state groups, the government told South Korean citizens that they were forbidden from accessing Burgess's Web site and any other Web pages about North Korea and warned that stern action would be taken against anyone who defied the law.

South Korea's actions marked the first time the country had taken their war with North Korea into cyberspace, and the story soon made international headlines. Internet users from all over the world began to descend on Burgess's Web site, eager to see what all the fuss was about.

As if public humiliation from South Korea weren't enough, Burgess himself was flooded with hundreds of e-mail messages from people asking him if he was a North Korean spy.

That turned out to be the last straw for Burgess. He pulled the plug on his Web site and replaced the materials with a message that read:

This site has not been censored by the administration of the University of Saskatchewan. This site, and all parts of it, have been removed by the account holder who originally posted it. The accout [*sic*] holder who posted it is no longer interested in keeping this site active, due to the hundreds of email messages which have been received with regard to it. Please

be so kind as to not bother the webmaster of this cluster, nor the account holder at ~ burgess with questions regarding this site.

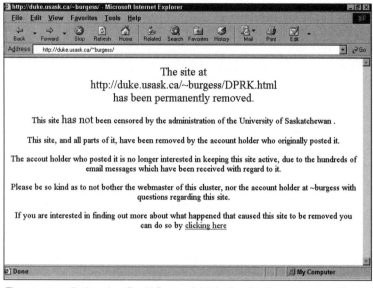

The message displayed on David Burgess's Web site after it was permanently shut down.

To this day, Burgess continues to deny that he has any political connections to North Korea.

Sources: Associated Press, *Daily Telegraph,* Reuters

Computer foul-ups are commonplace these days, but rarely are they legendary. In 1979, a Los Angeles resident named Robert Barbour found himself entangled in one of the most bizarre incidents I've ever come across. In fact, it's so bizarre, it's unlikely you could dream up this adventure even if you tried.

A LICENSE TO DRIVE YOU NUTS

California Department of Motor Vehicles, 1979

Barbour, like many Americans, was intrigued by the idea of getting a vanity license plate for his car, so he filled out an application form and sent it off to the California Department of Motor Vehicles (DMV). On the application form, he was asked to specify three different plate names, in case his first choice wasn't available. Barbour loved sailing and worked in the marine industry, so his first two choices were "Sailing" and "Boating." When it came to a third choice, Barbour didn't have one, so he wrote "No Plate" to indicate that he didn't want a personalized plate if he couldn't get his first or second choice.

When the DMV processed Barbour's application, they discovered that both the names "Sailing" and "Boating" had already been issued to other vehicles. However, "No Plate," which Barbour had printed beside his third choice, was available, so the DMV had the plates printed and sent to him.

Barbour couldn't believe his eyes when he received his personalized license plates in the mail. The DMV had interpreted his instructions literally and had sent him plates with the words "No Plate" written on them. Recognizing that he was in possession of a rather unusual collector's item, Barbour decided to keep the plates rather than return them. Little did he know that the fun was just beginning!

Several weeks after receiving his license plates, Barbour began to receive notices in the mail for overdue parking fines. Not just one or two notices, but dozens of them, and from all over the state. The parking fines didn't belong to Barbour, so why was he receiving them? Initially, Barbour was stumped at the avalanche of citations, but it wasn't long before he was able to put two and two together and unravel the mystery.

When issuing a ticket to a vehicle without license plates, a police officer would frequently scrawl "No plate" where the driver's license plate number was supposed to be written. This information was subsequently put into the state's computer system and the phrase "No plate" was entered where the vehicle's license plate number would normally appear.

If a ticket didn't get paid, the computer system would automatically generate an overdue notice and send it to the owner of the car. Because Barbour had license plates with the words "No Plate," the DMV computers were sending him all the overdue tickets where the police officer had written "No plate."

With his mystery solved, Barbour complained to the DMV and told them about his unusual predicament. In response, the DMV recommended that Barbour change his license plates if he wanted the parking fines to go away. But Barbour liked his unique plates and didn't want to give them up. Besides, he reasoned, this was the DMV's problem to solve, not his.

So Barbour embarked on an ambitious letter-writing campaign. Each time he received a letter about an unpaid parking ticket that didn't belong to him, he sent a form letter back to the DMV. It took two years, but Barbour's persistence eventually paid off. After receiving thousands of misdirected parking fines and spending over $300 on paper and postage, Barbour learned that the DMV was finally going to change their internal procedures for plateless vehicles. Police officers were going to be instructed to stop writing "No plate" on citations and start using the word "None" instead. But the story doesn't end here.

You guessed it—another California resident started receiving parking tickets in the mail that didn't belong to him. Some police officers had begun writing "Missing" on citations for vehicles that didn't have plates. A fellow named Andrew Burg was the unlucky guy who just happened to have a Honda with a personalized license plate that read "Missing" and he ended up receiving parking fines from all over the state. Unlike Barbour, he was able to clear up the confusion with a few letters to the appropriate jurisdictions.

Despite the aggravation caused by the "No Plate" fiasco, Barbour enjoyed his fifteen minutes of fame, and his story became legend around town. Once, when he was pulled over by the police, Barbour was worried that he'd be nabbed for an expired vehicle registration.

"The officer said he didn't really care about that," Barbour recalled in an interview with the *Los Angeles Times*. "He had heard about my car and license plates and just wanted to have his picture taken next to them. He brought out a camera from his patrol car and I took the picture for him."

Sources: *Los Angeles Times*, Snopes.com

More than forty years ago when Downy fabric softener was invented, the scientists at Procter & Gamble probably never imagined that their revolutionary product would one day be used to overturn the results in an election. But it happened in March 1996 during a vote in Polk County, Oregon.

A "SHOCKING" TALE

Polk County, Oregon, March 1996

The election results showed that a tax proposal had been defeated by an eight-vote margin. But election officials suspected that the computer hadn't tabulated the results properly, and a technician suggested they spray the carpet around the computer with Downy fabric softener. They did, and then they had the computer recalculate the vote. It turned out that the tax proposal had actually passed 806–727. The culprit was a bad case of static electricity. Believe it or not, the same static charge that causes a person to be zapped by an electric shock when he or she touches a hard surface or another person can actually play havoc with computer systems as well.

"Now we spray the Downy every time before we run the computers," said Valerie Unger, an Oregon election clerk who was interviewed by the *Wall Street Journal.* "It always smells really fresh." Procter & Gamble would no doubt be proud.

Sources: *Oregonian* (Portland), Procter & Gamble, *Wall Street Journal*

Political activists love the Internet because they can use it to thumb their noses at stodgy government bureaucrats who still see the world in black-and-white terms. Perhaps the most famous example of the Internet being used to flaunt a government order occurred in January 1996 when the French government tried to stop a politically sensitive hot potato from being disseminated in cyberspace. Needless to say, the Internet won and the French government was left with egg on their face.

CENSOR THIS!

Government of France, January 1996

This tale began in January 1996, when *Le Grand Secret*, a highly anticipated book about the late French president François Mitterand, arrived in bookstores across France. It had been the subject of much discussion across the country because the book, written by Mitterand's personal physician, alleged that the president had misled the public about the state of his health.

Within hours of *Le Grand Secret*'s being released to the public for the first time, the entire first-print run of 40,000 copies flew off the shelves. The very next day, Mitterand's family succeeded in getting a court order to ban any further sale of the book. They argued, and the court agreed, that the book had violated doctor-patient confidentiality.

No one expected what happened next, and it ignited a furious debate within France and around the world about censorship and freedom of speech.

Pascal Barbraud, the owner of an Internet café in France, decided to scan the entire 190-page book into his computer and post the whole thing on the World Wide Web. In 1996, this was quite a feat, and journalists were intrigued with Barbraud's bold accomplishment.

News of Barbraud's Web site quickly spread throughout the country and around the world. Within a matter of hours, his site was swamped with activity as people clamored to get a glimpse at the book the French government had tried so hard to conceal. At one point, Barbraud's Web site was receiving 1,000 requests an hour.

Media outlets, including news giant CNN, covered the story, further fueling the debate about how to ban a book on the Internet, a problem the world had never dealt with before on this large a scale.

A series of fascinating events ensued. The French police arrested Barbraud the day after the book appeared on his Web site.

Although the arrest was made on unrelated charges stemming from a child support case, the police readily admitted that all the publicity Barbraud was getting brought him to their attention again. Once that happened, many Internet users who had been closely following the events decided they could not sit by idly and watch the French government succeed in their attempts at censorship.

Aided by on-line discussion groups and e-mail, Internet users rallied behind Barbraud. Many people copied the entire book from Barbraud's Web site and uploaded the pages to their own Web sites.

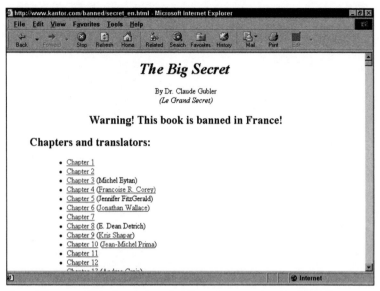

One of the many Web sites that carried the entire contents of Le Grand Secret.

But that was just the beginning. Since the book was written entirely in French, a group of volunteers mobilized on-line and began translating the book, page by page, into English. By April of 1996, English translations of *Le Grand Secret* began appearing all over the Internet, in countries far beyond the reach of French authorities. The French government's hands were now tied. They were powerless to stop the book from spreading, and free-speech activists around the world celebrated their victory.

There is no doubt that Barbraud's feat will go down in history as one of the most daring attempts ever to test the effectiveness of the courts in the age of computer technology, where entire books can be transmitted to millions of people at the touch of a button.

Sources: Agence France-Presse, Reuters, *Wall Street Journal*

BIZARRE CASE OF OVERBILLING

AN ABUSE OF POWER

Ladysmith-Emnambithi Municipality, South Africa, July 2002

For years, ninety-two-year-old Minnie Meyer of Colenso, South Africa, had been troubled by her unusually high electricity bills. She couldn't understand why her electricity meter was always "spinning like a top" even when no power was being consumed in her home. It was also odd that Meyer's neighbor, an avid cook who consumed a lot of electricity, paid less for her power than Meyer did.

Meyer's landlord, Leslie Swan, had investigated his tenant's complaints before but hadn't been able to come up with a logical explanation for the inflated hydro charges. Eventually, however, Swan became convinced that the mystery warranted further investigation, and so he asked the municipality to come out and install a new hydro meter.

It was then that an amazing discovery was made. When municipal workers showed up to replace Meyer's meter, they discovered that it was hooked up to three streetlights outside her flat. And that wasn't the only surprise. It appeared as though the streetlights had been connected to Meyer's electricity meter for the past thirty-five years! Nobody knows how this could have happened, but a spokesperson for the Ladysmith-Emnambithi Municipality blamed the wiring mishap on the former Colenso Town Council.

With Meyer's mystery solved, Swan demanded that the city refund at least some of his tenant's money. If that happens, it would no doubt be one of the biggest retroactive electricity refunds in South African history.

Source: *Cape Argus Newspaper* (South Africa)

t was the next best thing to a "Get Out of Jail Free" card. Nearly 200 inmates imprisoned by the Florida Department of Corrections pigged out on peanut M&M's, cheeseburgers, chocolate chip cookies, chewing tobacco, and other assorted goodies after hundreds of thousands of dollars were mistakenly deposited into their canteen accounts—the trust accounts that most inmates maintain so they can buy snack food, soap, and other hygiene products from the prison store.

FINDERS KEEPERS

Florida Department of Corrections, January–October 2000

As a result of a computer blunder, inmates at three Florida state prisons began receiving as much as $100 to $200 in extra money a *month*. It must have seemed like a gift from heaven, and the jailbirds quietly went on a spending spree, ordering everything from ice cream sandwiches to chili dogs.

The inmates' incredible windfall started in January 2000 and miraculously went undetected for at least ten months. The screwup was only discovered when some of the inmates began complaining that money was vanishing from their canteen accounts. The prison launched an investigation and was stunned when they discovered that a system problem caused money to be taken from some inmates and was giving money to others. According to a corrections spokesperson, the glitch occurred during a change in computer systems.

Officials quickly put a halt to the free handouts, and inmates who benefited from the glitch were ordered to start repaying the money they had previously spent. Since many of the inmates didn't have any savings to draw from, the prison started deducting money from what their families sent them.

Prison officials vowed they would get all the money back.

Sources: Florida Department of Corrections, *Orlando Sentinel*

> You would think the president of the United States
> would know better.

THE JOKE THAT BOMBED

U.S. President Ronald Reagan, August 1984

On Saturday, August 11, 1984, President Ronald Reagan was preparing for his weekly radio address from his ranch near Santa Barbara, California. It was the middle of the 1984 presidential campaign.

To test the sound on the microphone, President Reagan decided to tell a joke instead of using a more traditional voice-check like "Testing one/two/three." Speaking into the microphone, Reagan quipped: "My fellow Americans, I'm pleased to tell you today that I've signed legislation that would outlaw Russia forever. We begin bombing in five minutes." The remark was caught on tape by at least two news organizations that happened to be recording at the time.

Reagan's off-the-cuff comments ignited controversy around the world, especially in Europe, where the incident was front-page news on August 13. Reaction was swift and unforgiving.

In West Germany, for instance, the Social Democratic Party called Reagan "an irresponsible old man." In London, *The Standard* called the incident "a joke which has turned into a serious embarrassment." And in the Netherlands, the Teletekst news service snidely remarked, "Hopefully, the man tests his missiles more carefully." Meanwhile, in the Soviet Union, where Reagan's joke had raised questions about the future of U.S.–Soviet relations, officials labeled Reagan's remarks as "hostile."

To make matters worse, both CBS and NBC decided to air Reagan's remarks on their evening news broadcasts. For their part, CBS News had initially decided they were not going to broadcast a tape of Reagan's comments because they were made off the record. However, according to CBS's director of communications, CBS elected to reverse that decision because "everybody was running with the story."

Although Reagan's remarks were evidently tongue-in-cheek, many critics thought otherwise and Reagan's true intentions were the subject of intense debate across the country.

Later that week, Reagan finally broke his silence on the matter and told a group of business leaders at the White House that he was indeed "not going to bomb Russia in the next five minutes." It was Reagan's first attempt to make light of his original joke in public.

Eventually, the furor died down, but Reagan's voice-test gaffe would go down in the history books as one of the most memorable moments of his presidency.

Sources: Associated Press, UPI, *Washington Post*, other news services

President Reagan's ill-timed remark about bombing the Russians was not the only political slipup involving an open microphone.

A MAJOR·LEAGUE BLUNDER

Governor George W. Bush, September 2000

On September 4, 2000, then governor George W. Bush was campaigning in Naperville, Illinois, with his running mate, Dick Cheney. Prior to making a campaign speech, Bush leaned over to Cheney and made a rude comment about a *New York Times* reporter who had been covering the campaign. Unaware that his microphone was turned on, Bush remarked, "There's Adam Clymer, major-league a****** from the *New York Times.*" Cheney whispered back, "Oh yeah, he is, big time."

Neither Bush nor Cheney realized their private conversation was actually being broadcast to the throngs of supporters gathered at the event—and to the media.

When Al Gore, Bush's Democratic opponent, learned about Bush's foot-in-the-mouth gaffe, he jokingly made reference to it during a campaign speech in Pittsburgh. "I want to thank the working press corps who are working on Labor Day," he said.

George W. Bush with Dick Cheney on Labor Day, 2000.

Later asked to comment on his remarks, Bush said, "I regret that it made it to the airwaves." Cheney was tight-lipped as well. "The governor made a private comment to me," he said. "It was a private comment, and I don't plan to say anything about it."

At the following day's White House press briefing, John Podesta, President Clinton's chief of staff, joked with reporters. "Is this mike on?" asked Podesta at the beginning of the news conference. "You can never be too careful these days."

Sources: ABC News, Associated Press

Everyone dreads getting paperwork from the government. So you can imagine how a California dentist felt when 16,000 (yes, that's sixteen *thousand*) tax forms, each in its own envelope, were delivered to his San Diego–area office in September 1996.

"YOU'VE GOT MAIL"

State of California, September 1996

The tidal wave of mail was caused by a computer glitch in a state government computer, and it's possibly the largest amount of mail ever delivered to a single address as a result of a computer error.

The error occurred when a software package the government was using to produce address labels had trouble reading the word "suite." The word was abbreviated throughout the government's database as "su," but the software package was only programmed to recognize the abbreviation "ste." Normally, that wouldn't have been a problem because the software was supposed to jump back to the previous line in the address when it encountered a word it couldn't understand. But the previous line on the dentist's address contained a foreign spelling of a word, and the software became stuck. The program literally went haywire after that, printing out the dentist's address over and over again, until it had created 16,000 address labels.

The dentist, who was not identified by the government, reportedly phoned in to report the unusual mail delivery. The tax forms were promptly picked up and hauled back to their origin in Sacramento.

Humorous as it was, the incident was a relatively minor one for the State of California, which, at the time, mailed out over 68 million pieces of mail to employers a year. The department affected by the glitch was confident it wouldn't happen again. "We alerted the postal authorities and they corrected the problem with what they call a 'software patch,'" said a government spokesperson quoted by the *Sacramento Bee*. The total cost of postage for the accidental mailing was $4,064.

Source: *Sacramento Bee*

PART 7

MISCELLANEOUS MARVELS, FANTASTIC FEATS, AND OTHER ODDITIES

here are only seven great wonders of the world, but if scores of Internet users had their way, there would probably be eight.

RINGING UP A CONTROVERSY

The Mojave Telephone Booth Project, 1997–2000

The unlikely candidate is a battered and age-ridden phone booth that was installed at the junction of two dirt roads in the middle of California's Mojave Desert. The phone had been placed there decades ago to serve local miners, but by the late 1990s, it looked more like a prop from an old Western movie than a public utility. The windows were shot out, the phone book was gone, and the door was missing. But the phone still worked and residents in the sparsely populated area occasionally used the booth to make phone calls.

The booth would probably have remained in the desert for several more decades had a Phoenix-based computer consultant named

Godfrey Daniels not stumbled across it one day in 1997. While reading
Wig Out!, a magazine produced by one of his favorite rock-and-roll
bands, Godfrey noticed a letter to the editor from a reader who had
discovered "a small dot with the word 'telephone' beside it" on a map of
the Mojave Desert.

Intrigued, the reader had driven out to the remote area and was
amazed to discover that there was indeed a working telephone in the
middle of the windswept desert. He included the actual telephone number
for the phone booth in his letter, warning other readers to "let it ring"
for a long time if they wanted a response.

Godfrey's curiosity was piqued by the letter and he became
fascinated with this telephone booth that was so far removed from
civilization. He began calling the booth every day and taping his calls,
hoping that one day a real person might answer. Then it happened.
On June 20, 1997, Godfrey was shocked to encounter a busy signal
on the line.

"Either there was something wrong with the line—which I thought
most likely—or there was a real human being talking on the phone
in the middle of the Mojave Desert!" he explains on his Web site,
DeuceofClubs.com.

His heart racing, Godfrey kept trying the line and eventually
it rang. A woman answered, and Godfrey entered into an excited
conversation with her. He eventually learned that she lived in the
Mojave Desert and that she occasionally used the telephone booth to
make calls.

Following his first successful connection to this phone booth in the
middle of nowhere, Godfrey couldn't stop thinking about the phone.
He took several trips out to the desert to visit the booth and he began
chronicling his adventures on a Web site he created.

The famous Mojave telephone booth.

Word of Godfrey's Web site quickly spread around the Internet and before long the Mojave telephone booth had achieved the type of cult status that is normally reserved for television shows like *The Simpsons* and *Survivor.*

People from all over the world began to flock to the Mojave Desert just to have their pictures taken with this unique desert landmark. For those unable to make the trip, they did the next best thing and called the booth's phone number to see who they might reach at the other end. Simply making a connection with the world's loneliest phone booth was a surreal experience for most people. And it was more surreal if someone actually answered. "Oh my God, I can't believe it! Somebody answered! There's actually somebody out there!" one caller told a reporter from the *Los Angeles Times* who was answering calls at the booth one day.

The area soon became overrun with curiosity seekers. At its peak, the phone began receiving around 200 calls a day. Romances even blossomed—one visitor met his fiancée there and planned to get married at the site.

The media got caught up in the frenzy, too, and stories about the phone booth began to appear in newspapers across the United States. A Denver radio station offered $1,000 to the first listener who drove out to the phone booth and called back to the station. Television stations got a piece of the action as well. Even the *NBC Nightly News* broadcast a story. And on the Web, where this whole craze initially began, countless on-line shrines devoted to the booth began to spring up as people trekked into the desert to see the phone with their very own eyes.

"I've passed that old phone booth just about every day for more than twenty years now and I've never given it as much as a second thought," said Charlie Wilcox, a local resident who was interviewed by the *Los Angeles Times*. "And I'll be damned. Now it's a celebrity."

As more and more people converged on the desert in search of the famous phone booth, the National Park Service became increasingly concerned. Almost overnight, the area had become a major tourist attraction and there were worries about people becoming lost or stranded. There were also some safety and environmental concerns. Litter was reportedly accumulating in the area, vegetation was being damaged, and at least one campfire had apparently gotten out of control. Although the severity of these issues was disputed by supporters of the phone booth, the National Park Service's patience with the phone's newfound notoriety eventually ran out.

In May 2000, Pacific Bell technicians were dispatched to the desert, where they quietly dismantled the celebrity phone. "While the phone and its location proved to be a novelty for some in recent months, the increased public traffic had a negative impact on the desert environment in the nation's newest national park," said a terse statement issued by the Park Service. And with that, the phone was gone. A few concrete blocks as well as the phone's base were all that remained at the site.

The National Park Service's decision sparked immediate outrage—and sadness—among supporters of the phone booth (including the author of this book). "It stinks. There is absolutely no reason for it. Isn't that what a park is for—for people to visit?" said local resident Lorene Caffee in an interview with the *Desert Dispatch*. Other fans took to the Web and directed their anger at Mary Martin, the superintendent of the Mojave National Preserve.

"No one, not even Mary Martin, superintendent of the Mojave National Preserve, or her boss, John Reynolds, quite knows the depth of what we lost on that fateful May morning in 2000 when, at the request of Preserve administration, a Pacific Bell truck lumbered up Aiken Mine Road and carried away an icon that had existed for longer than most locals can remember," wrote a supporter named Doug Arendt on his Web site. "An icon that had

A picture of the Mojave telephone booth site in 2000, after the phone booth had been hauled away by Pacific Bell.

existed long before the Mojave National Preserve was ever conceived. An icon that probably existed when Mary and John were playing with toy telephones. An icon that will forever be missed."

Godfrey mounted an immediate campaign on his Web site, encouraging people to write the U.S. Congress as well as the National Park Service, but the parties responsible for uprooting the phone booth have refused to reconsider their decision. If you want to protest the booth's removal, names and telephone numbers can be found on Gottfried's Web site at www.deuceof clubs.com/moj/mojave.htm.

A memorial was erected at the former site of the Mojave telephone booth by an unknown individual.

Although the letter-writing campaign seems to have fallen on deaf ears, the phone's legend still lives on, both in cyberspace and at its former physical location in the middle of nowhere.

Sources: Doug Arendt (www.geocities.com/destrip), *Desert Dispatch, DeuceofClubs.com, Los Angeles Times*

arbra Streisand may be a great female vocalist, but she ain't no Shakespeare expert. That was evident in late September 2002, when she performed at a lavish Democratic Party fund raiser in Hollywood and voiced her opposition to President Bush's war policy.

OUT OF TUNE
WITH HISTORY

Barbra Streisand, September 2002

To make her point to the thousands of Democratic Party supporters who had gathered at the event, she quoted what she thought was a beautiful passage from Shakespeare.

"You know, really good artists have a way of being relevant in their time . . . but great artists are relevant at any time," she said. Then she proceeded to read the following quote:

Beware the leader who bangs the drums of war in order to whip up the citizenry into a patriotic fervor, for patriotism is indeed a double-edged sword. It both emboldens the blood, just as it narrows the mind. And when the drums of war have

reached a fever pitch and the blood boils with hate and the mind has closed, the leader will have no need in seizing the rights of the citizenry. Rather, the citizenry, infused with fear and blinded with patriotism, will offer up all of their rights unto the leader, and gladly so. How do I know? For this is what I have done. And I am Caesar.

"Imagine that was written over 400 years ago," Streisand marveled to the audience. "It's amazing how history without consciousness is destined to repeat itself."

Unbeknownst to Barbra, the passage was never written by Shakespeare. In fact, it was nothing more than an Internet hoax that had been circulating on the Web for months. The quotation had been given to Streisand by a friend who had discovered it on the Internet, credited to Shakespeare's play *Julius Caesar.*

Streisand's amusing blunder made headlines around the world after Internet gossip columnist Matt Drudge broke the story on his Web site. "Today the woman who sang 'Second Hand Rose' got burned by second-hand prose," he beamed.

Streisand tried to put the best possible light on her blunder by praising the quotation for its powerful message. "The authorship of this is important. But it doesn't detract from the fact that the words themselves are powerful and true and beautifully written," she said in a statement that was posted on her Web site.

She went on to suggest that the author of the hoax had a promising career ahead of him or her. "Whoever wrote this is damn talented and should be writing their own play," she remarked.

Lindsay Kaplan, a professor of English at Georgetown University, said the talented crooner should have known better. Kaplan said the passage contained words that didn't even exist in sixteenth-century

England—an obvious sign the writing was bogus. "First of all, words like 'patriotism' and 'citizenry' were not even in use when Shakespeare was alive," she told the *Washington Post*. "Beyond that, it's just a very clumsy piece of writing."

Sources: Agence France-Presse, Associated Press, Drudge Report, *Globe and Mail*, *New York Post*, Reuters, *Washington Post*

> f you want to create a press release that *really* gets
> noticed, try issuing a press release with only one word
> in it. Believe it or not, it's actually been done before.

THE LAST WORD

Amazon.com, November 1998

n 1998, on-line booksellers
Amazon.com and Barnes & Noble were engaged in a bitter feud over
their respective business practices. During a single week that year, the
two industry titans battled it out in an amusing series of news releases,
the likes of which are rarely seen in the business world.

Following a deal by Barnes & Noble to spend $600 million to
purchase Ingram Books, the largest wholesale book distributor in the
United States, Amazon.com issued a statement suggesting that Barnes
& Noble's move would undoubtedly "raise industry-wide concerns."
The statement ended with a parting shot from Amazon.com founder
and chief executive officer Jeff Bezos. "Worry not . . . Goliath is always
in range of a good slingshot," he said.

Barnes & Noble wasted no time in firing back with their own press
release, stating, "We suppose you know a Goliath when you see one.

Your company is now worth more than Barnes & Noble, Borders and all of the independent bookstores combined. . . . Slingshots and potshots should not be part of your arsenal."

Not wanting to let Barnes & Noble have the last word, Amazon shot back in a release titled "Amazon.com Issues Statement Regarding BarnesandNoble.com's Statement Regarding Amazon.com's Statement about Barnes & Noble, Inc." The press release, shown below, contained a single word: "Oh."

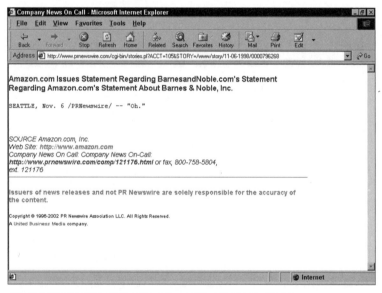

Amazon.com's single-word press release about BarnesandNoble.com.

It was the first single-word press release in the history of the business world!

Sources: Amazon.com, Barnes & Noble, *Wall Street Journal*

> Students at one of England's most exclusive schools got more than they bargained for when they sat down to write a mock school exam in May 2002. And it wasn't the exam that caught them off guard, it was the sideshow at the front of the room.

INDECENCY 101

Marlborough College, Wiltshire, England, May 2002

It seems that the teacher presiding over the exam got a little bored and decided to pass his time by viewing adult porn on his laptop computer. Watching an adult video in a school classroom is bad enough, but the teacher made a second critical mistake. He left his laptop plugged into the big screen at the front of the room, and everything the teacher viewed on his computer monitor was projected onto the large white screen behind him.

According to England's *Daily Mail,* one of the students in the classroom happened to look up during the exam and saw pictures of naked women on the screen. She reportedly gasped in horror and left the exam room to find a staff member. The teacher, now acutely aware of his gaffe, frantically scrambled to remove the explicit content from the overhead screen as amused students watched in disbelief.

The teacher was placed on leave and the school launched an immediate investigation into the incident. There was no word on whether he would be "stripped" of his job.

Sources: *Daily Mail, Times* (London)

When you have something that someone else wants, it's amazing what you can get just by asking for it. Just ask Glenn Hurst of Alberta, Canada. In 1996, he orchestrated one of the most memorable domain name sales in the history of the Internet by negotiating a deal that was both clever and bold.

POTATO POWER

Potato Growers of Alberta, December 1996

In 1996, Glenn was working for a trade organization in Canada called the Potato Growers of Alberta. Besides his passion for potatoes, Glenn was fond of music, and he ran a small deejay service on the side, offering his disc jockey expertise to weddings and corporate functions.

In the mid-1990s, the potato growers, led by Glenn, registered the Internet domain name PGA.com and subsequently created a site on the World Wide Web. Not long after the site was launched, the potato growers noticed an unusually high amount of traffic on their site. While the attention their cyberspace outpost was receiving was flattering, it soon became apparent that many of the visitors had come looking for golf information and tour schedules, not potato recipes.

It didn't take long to figure out where all the misdirected visitors were coming from. As luck would have it, the Potato Growers of Alberta shared the same initials as the Professional Golfers' Association of America, the largest golf organization in the world and the organizer of prestigious golf tournaments such as the Ryder Cup and the PGA Championship. Web surfers who had typed www.pga.com into their Web browsers hoping to find golf advice were surprised, and you might say dismayed, to receive baking tips instead.

The Professional Golfers' Association of America, meanwhile, was well aware of the fact that their preferred Internet address had been snatched up by the potato people in Canada. Although they had already secured various addresses for their Web site, including *www.pga.org* and *www.pgatour.com,* their goal was to somehow persuade the Potato Growers of Alberta to relinquish ownership of PGA.com. With that objective in mind, the golf association approached the Potato Growers of Alberta in early 1996 to see if they could come to an amicable agreement to transfer ownership of the domain name. When the PGA came knocking, Glenn Hurst at the potato growers organization took charge of the matter and commenced negotiations.

Not long after discussions began, a deal was struck to transfer ownership of the PGA.com domain name to the Professional Golfers' Association. In a sweet deal favoring the potato growers organization, the golfers agreed to pay around $35,000 for the domain name. But that was only the tip of the iceberg.

Because the Web site for Glenn's deejay service was part of the PGA.com Internet site, Glenn was worried that his customers would be unable to find his business once ownership of the Web address was transferred to the golf association.

Glenn was determined to protect his business, so he came up with a rather interesting solution. You might say that Glenn and his group of potato growers were pushing their luck, but in an amusing and unprecedented twist that was part of the negotiated settlement, the golf association agreed to advertise Glenn's personal deejay service on their Web site.

On December 1, 1996, the Professional Golfers' Association of America officially took over ownership of the PGA.com domain name and the Potato Growers of Alberta began using a new Internet address—www.potatonet.com.

True to their promise, the PGA, one of the most prestigious professional sporting organizations in the world, began advertising a deejay service on their popular Web site.

In the end, all parties were happy with the final settlement. The golf association got the Internet address they wanted, the potato growers organization got $35,000 to offset the cost of changing their Web address and reprinting all of their stationery, and a small-business owner in Alberta got a once-in-a-lifetime deal that briefly saw his deejay service promoted on one of the busiest golf sites in the entire world.

Sources: Glenn Hurst, *Toronto Star*

In October 2002, Canadian author Yann Martel accomplished a feat that is unique in the annals of Britain's prestigious Man Booker Prize for fiction. He managed to win the $77,000 (U.S.) prize before the judges had even met!

"BOOKED FOR TROUBLE"

London, England, October 2002

The Thursday before the jury was scheduled to meet, a press release appeared on the Booker Prize Web site announcing that Martel's novel *Life of Pi* had been declared the winner. This prompted a flurry of bets for Martel's book with William Hill, Britain's largest bookie, which was taking wagers for the award. Martel suddenly became the clear favorite to win and his book's odds jumped ahead of all the other novels on the shortlist. Other candidates for the literary honor included Canadian authors Carol Shields and Rohinton Mistry, Australian novelist Tim Winton, Irish author William Trevor, and British writer Sarah Waters.

The rush of bets on Martel's novel caught the attention of William Hill officials, who became alarmed when they learned that the contest was apparently over. "We were baffled by a string of bets for the Martel book, several of them stakes of one hundred pounds at a time, and then concerned when we heard that the book had already been announced as the winner," said a spokesperson for the bookie.

Booker Prize officials quickly removed the press release and explained that the announcement had been made in error. They said that press releases for each of the six short-listed candidates had been prepared in advance, and Martel's release was mistakenly published on the Web site.

"One of the releases was being sent to a development Web site as a test, but unfortunately it was accidentally sent to a site which could be seen by the public," said an award spokesperson. "It just happened to be the Martel press release, as his name is first of the six alphabetically."

Martel was good-humored about the gaffe and hoped it was a sign of things to come. "Let's just hope it's an omen," he joked with Canada's *National Post* newspaper in an interview. "It really was purely a mistake. It's just because I was the first one on the list because I was closest to the letter A. If I do win, maybe the logic is that whoever is highest up on the list wins the prize, so I suppose Aaron Aardvark will win the next Booker Prize."

The error immediately created suspicion that perhaps the literary contest was somehow rigged, but Booker officials said that was impossible because the judges hadn't even met yet to deliberate. Ironically, Martel was declared the official winner five days later.

Sources: BBC, Canadian Press, *National Post,* Reuters

> huck Barr of Jamestown, California, has a unique perspective to offer when it comes to paying down the national debt. That's because he knows exactly what it's like to be facing a multitrillion-dollar bill.

ONE "FINE" MESS

Tuolumne County Library (California), January 2001

In early 2001, Barr received a letter from his library, dated January 20, telling him to pay a fine of nearly $40,000,000,000,000 for a damaged book that he had borrowed. That's 40 *trillion* dollars, almost seven times the national debt of the United States.

"Library records show that the following charges have not been paid," the letter read. "Please resolve these charges at the circulation desk as soon as possible. If you have already contacted the library concerning these outstanding charges, please disregard this notice." The notice showed that Barr's account was in arrears by $39,949,000,620,214.

"I had to put the commas in to figure out how much it was," Barr told the *Modesto Bee,* the local newspaper, where his story was front-page news. "It sure made my heating bill look small." When I reached him at his home in Jamestown, just southeast of Sacramento, Barr joked that he's still trying to pay the darn thing off.

The size of the library fine had local politicians rejoicing and fanta-sizing how they were going to spend the money. One county official hoped some of the funds would be used to help the region's financially strapped hospital.

Of course, they were only dreams, because Barr's notice was nothing more than a surreal computer glitch. The library told him that the overdue notice got issued when a book's bar code inadvertently got entered into the "amount due" field on their computer system, causing the fourteen-digit fine to be tabulated. The library canceled the fine and told Barr not to worry about it.

Barr told the *Modesto Bee* that he wished the library had sent him a trillion-dollar check instead of a trillion-dollar fine. "But then again," he said, "that would have been about as worthless as the bill."

Sources: Chuck Barr, *Modesto Bee*

very now and again, you come across a story that just makes you shake your head in disbelief. The following tale is one of those stories. It involves a woman from Geneseo, Illinois, who got herself stuck in a newspaper box. That in itself is hard to believe, but even more astonishing was the reaction of the local Wal-Mart store, which initially refused to free the trapped woman on the grounds that it would violate their store policy.

BOXED IN

Wal-Mart, Geneseo, Illinois, March 2002

att Gergeni, a reporter at the *Moline Dispatch* in Illinois, first broke this incredible story, which provoked howls of laughter across the United States and left Wal-Mart executives red-faced with embarrassment.

The woman, who prefers to remain anonymous, was about to enter Wal-Mart when she decided to grab a copy of the local newspaper, the *Moline Dispatch,* from the vending machine outside the store. She put some money into the coin slot and retrieved the newspaper. But before she could stand upright and move away from the newspaper box, the spring-operated door accidentally slammed shut, catching the cords on the hood of her jacket and trapping them in the box.

"I tried to pull them (the strings) out of the machine, but the little metal balls on the ends just wouldn't come out," the woman told the *Moline Dispatch*. With part of her hood stuck inside the newspaper box, she was hunched over in an uncomfortable position, unable to lift her body fully upright.

Having had surgery on one of her shoulders, the seventy-three-year-old woman was also unable to wiggle out of her coat, so she sat there in the cold waiting for someone to walk by and help her. No one came. She called for help, but no one heard her cries.

Then a young woman walked by and the trapped woman got her attention. Could she run inside and get an employee to bring out some change, open the newspaper box, and get her out? The young woman obliged, and a few minutes later she emerged from the store. The trapped woman was relieved that someone was finally going to be able to get her free. But the news was disappointing. Wal-Mart had told the young woman they couldn't help her because the newspaper box wasn't their property.

By this time, the elderly woman had been stuck in the newspaper box for about five minutes and she was beginning to lose her cool.

What happened next is truly unbelievable—and incomprehensible. In an interview with reporter John Kass of the *Chicago Tribune,* parts of which are excerpted below with the permission of the paper, the woman recalled the incredible turn of events.

A Wal-Mart clerk emerged from the store and reiterated the store's position on the matter. "There's nothing we can do. We can't tamper with the newspaper box," the Wal-Mart clerk reportedly told the trapped woman. "We don't give refunds. It's not our box. We can't tamper with it."

"I don't want you to tamper with it," replied the woman, who was not able to look at the clerk, since she was hunched over, staring at the ground. All she wanted was someone to put fifty cents in the box so she could get herself out.

"Just open the machine," the woman pleaded. "Just like you're buying the paper! Free me!"

The Wal-Mart employee wouldn't budge. "No, no," she said. "No refunds. We'll have to call down to the *Dispatch.* We'll have to get one of their employees to get a key and open it."

The woman was stunned. "What? You're going to leave me standing here?"

The Wal-Mart clerk replied, "Well, there's nothing we can do."

The clerk walked away and left the seventy-three-year-old woman in her hunched-over position, trapped by the newspaper box. "That's when I lost it," recalled the woman to the *Chicago Tribune.* "The gal, she's preaching to me about not giving out refunds, and I'm stuck there for twenty minutes."

"I'm screaming, 'I don't want a refund!' I yelled, 'You mean to tell me you're going to call the *Dispatch*? You get in that store right now and get some quarters and come here and open this machine!'"

The trapped woman kept begging for help and eventually the Wal-Mart clerk agreed to free her from the box. The clerk brought out two quarters but had the nerve to tell the woman she wanted the money back.

When the woman was finally freed, her first act was to go into the Wal-Mart and pay back the fifty cents that the clerk had reluctantly donated to secure her freedom. Then she went home to nurse her sore back. Wal-Mart probably thought that was the end of the matter. The woman was free, and all was well. Well, nothing could be farther from the truth.

News of the woman's ordeal quickly spread around the town. The *Moline Dispatch* wrote a story about the incident, which led to another story in the *Chicago Tribune,* and soon Wal-Mart officials were having to answer some tough questions about their inhumane treatment of an elderly woman. How could they leave her stuck in a newspaper box when a mere fifty cents would have secured her freedom?

When the woman's daughter heard about her mother's ordeal and Wal-Mart's evident lack of common courtesy, she was furious. She stormed into the Wal-Mart store and slammed a five-dollar bill on the counter. "[My mother] left them five dollars," the woman told the *Chicago Tribune.* "That'll buy out the next ten people who get caught in the newspaper machine."

So what did Wal-Mart have to say about the shameful behavior of their employee? "This is not how we do business," said Sharon Weber, a Wal-Mart public relations officer who was quoted by the *Moline Dispatch.* "The store manager will be getting in touch with the woman to offer an apology for how the matter was handled and will do anything that he can to make it up to her."

The woman subsequently received a letter of apology and a twenty-five-dollar gift certificate from the manager of the Wal-Mart store. The newspaper that owned the vending machine, the *Moline Dispatch*, offered her a free month's subscription to their newspaper to compensate her for the ordeal.

Meanwhile, news of the woman's horrible experience landed on the desk of Dave Barry, the popular syndicated humorist, who used the amusing incident as fodder for his weekly column. In an article about the crisis facing the newspaper industry, he argued that the Illinois woman's experience highlighted some potential future uses for newspaper vending machines:

"If a relatively stupid, spring-operated newspaper vending machine can catch and hold a customer, imagine the results we'd get if we equipped these machines with computers, motors, wheels, stun guns, etc.," he wrote. "We have the technology to make a vending machine that can chase prospective readers for miles, knock down their doors, and refuse to take no for an answer."

Dave Barry may have been onto something, but the woman from Illinois who inspired his idea wasn't going to have any part of it. "I'm never going near that box again," she vowed to the *Chicago Tribune*.

Sources: *Chicago Tribune*, Matt Gergeni, *Miami Herald*, *Moline Dispatch*

PHOTOGRAPHY AND GRAPHIC CREDITS

Every effort has been made to correctly attribute all the materials reproduced and/or used in this book. If any errors have been made, we will be happy to correct them in future editions.

"Best On-Line Revenge for Poor Customer Service": PowerPoint slides courtesy of Shane Atchison and Tom Farmer, ZAAZ, Inc., Seattle, Washington, www.zaaz.com.

"Most Financially Harmful E-Mail Message": Stock graphic data provided by Standard & Poor's ComStock.

"Biggest Public Relations Frenzy Caused by a Customer E-Mail": Cartoon by Dan McHale. Used by permission.

"Strangest Explanation for a Check Error": Photo courtesy of *The Journal*, Crosby, North Dakota.

"Biggest Billing Mishap by a Major Hotel Chain": MasterCard statement courtesy of Tom Spears.

"Biggest Goof on a Water Bill": Photograph by Brian Diggs, *Austin-American Statesman*. Used by permission.

"Biggest Trading Gaffe Caused by an Elbow": Illustration courtesy of Ken Ellis, *Houston Chronicle*.

"Strangest Discovery by an Airport Metal Detector": CT scan courtesy of Luvera Law Firm, Seattle, Washington.

"Most Unlikely Place for a Cell Phone": X-ray graphic courtesy of *The Register*.

"Strangest Assembly Line Glitch at a Cereal Plant": *Jeopardy!* graphic courtesy of Sony Pictures Television.

"Most Offensive Bill from a Phone Company": Telephone bill courtesy of James Storrie.

"Biggest On-Line Media Gaffe in a Major Court Case": Harry Truman photograph courtesy of the Canadian Press/the Associated Press. Pathfinder images courtesy of Time, Inc.

"Strangest Sight on a News Agency Photograph": Bert/bin Laden photograph courtesy of Agence France-Presse.

"Most Successful Disruption of a Network News Broadcast": Cartoon provided by Patrick Corrigan, *Toronto Star*.

"Most Humorous Spoof of a Government Organization": Correspondence courtesy of the Yes Men (theyesmen.org)

"Most Potentially Lethal Open-Mike Gaffe by a Politician": Cartoon by Adrian Raeside, *Victoria Times-Colonist*. Used by permission.

"Most Embarrassing Open-Mike Gaffe by a Politician": Photograph courtesy of the Canadian Press/the Associated Press.

ABOUT THE AUTHOR

Rick Broadhead is an award-winning entrepreneur, literary agent, best-selling author, and professional speaker who has written or cowritten more than thirty books. He can be reached by e-mail at *rickb@rickbroadhead.com* or on the World Wide Web at *www.rickbroadhead.com*.

DO YOU HAVE A STORY TO TELL?

If you have a funny, embarrassing, or remarkable story that you think would qualify for inclusion in a future edition of this book, I'd love to hear from you. Please send me all the pertinent details along with any supporting evidence or documentation.

Of course, I'd also like to hear from you if you are aware of an incident that "trumps" any of the feats described in this book.

I can be reached by e-mail at *rickb@rickbroadhead.com* or you can write to me in care of my publisher:

Rick Broadhead
Dear Valued Customer, You Are a Loser
c/o Andrews McMeel Publishing
4520 Main Street
Kansas City, Missouri 64111
U.S.A.

I look forward to hearing from you!